T0375585

Hell,
and the
Lake of Fire

Hell's Ending

JIM CATES

WESTBOW
PRESS®
A DIVISION OF THOMAS NELSON
& ZONDERVAN

WestBow Press books may be ordered through booksellers or by contacting:

WestBow Press
A Division of Thomas Nelson & Zondervan
1663 Liberty Drive
Bloomington, IN 47403
www.westbowpress.com
844-714-3454

Scripture quotations marked KJV are taken from the King James Version.

ISBN: 979-8-3850-3625-7 (sc)
ISBN: 979-8-3850-3627-1 (hc)
ISBN: 979-8-3850-3626-4 (e)

Library of Congress Control Number: 2024921860

Print information available on the last page.

WestBow Press rev. date: 10/16/2024

Contents

Introduction

Years ago, while I was in my forties, I decided to go back to college and pursue a degree in pastoral studies. I looked into and investigated a biblical college in a town close to where I lived and, after a lot of prayer, decided to attend. I enrolled and started classes.

As days, weeks, and months passed, I became like a small child in a candy store. I could not get enough knowledge about the Scriptures. The more I learned about God's amazing words, the more I wanted to learn. It was exciting, and I loved it. Even the tests and those research papers, which many hated, excited me. It seemed like the more I studied, the more I got to know about God and His amazing love. And it stirred my soul tremendously.

I enjoyed all the classes and loved being around those classmates who, like me, had a zeal about learning all we could about our Lord. We often challenged each other about what we learned in our classes. We had many discussions on several topics in the Scriptures that normally would not come up in our churches.

As time went on, I began to notice that many words in the Scriptures had different meanings than what I was taught, as a young Christian, in both the New Testament and the Old. In the differences, I saw things that amazed and puzzled me at the same time. I questioned myself as to why I had only now begun to see them. *Why have they been hidden from my eyes until now?*

These new facts and ideas stirred my heart and gave me a brand-new light and insight into God's words, which I had never seen or studied before. It filled me with awe and wonder to see how the

Greek and Hebrew words of the original text shed a new light on the Scriptures that I never knew existed. Here were meanings that I had never imagined, and that excited me greatly.

I was fascinated when I saw how many of those original meanings of certain Greek and Hebrew words changed their contexts so greatly that I began to wonder: why was the original text different from today's translations? Why were they not the same? What was the reasoning behind it? Why the difference?

I found myself questioning the words that the translators into English used instead of providing the correct and true pronunciation and meanings. Why did they not use the correct translations of certain words? Of course, later I found out that dominant people such as King James and others in power influenced them. But still I wondered if they knew they were keeping the Word of God from being completely understood. How many millions of Christians never saw what I was now seeing? What was the reason that these facts were hidden? Certain words in Scripture, and their original meanings, which I was learning, brought out in me a spark of interest that changed my life completely. They moved me to want to learn and study more, to teach more, and especially to love God more.

As time went on, I wondered why God allowed certain facts to be hidden. What was the reason behind it all? Why did the translations fail to provide the correct meaning of these words as the years rolled on? Oh, sometimes you do see the true meanings. (It may be in the margins or at the bottom of the page, but it is not very noticeable if it is there.) And quite often, you will never see the correct meaning of certain words.

Again, what is the reasoning behind not providing the correct translation? What was the reasoning for not being educated about the true meaning of God's words? I have heard excuses, quite often, over the years, that the preachers and pastors are the ones who are supposed to do the educating, not the translations. Which is true to some measure, but why were the translators not providing the original meanings of these words openly and plainly? Were Satan and his forces behind this? Or did God want certain facts and ideas to be hidden, because humankind could not fathom them?

But in studying history, I came to realize that many teachers, preachers, and pastors were never taught. But still, I wondered why certain things about God's amazing Word were hidden in the translations. Why would God allow this? What was the reasoning? Where were the educators and teachers? Why were certain truths never brought out into the light? And if they were, they were looked down upon. I have seen that in my lifetime.

Even in my generation, I have noticed, as in the past, that many of our preachers and pastors are and were never exposed to or taught about the true meanings. Why is it? In most of our churches today, I find that many of our preachers and pastors today are not educated. That's not a bad thing, but in order to teach, you need to know what you are teaching about. I have seen many self-educated preachers, and pastors, and they are good teachers, but I have learned over the years that, for most men and women, experience and education are the best teachers. It does not make any difference; education is essential and vital for those who teach God's Word, whether self-educated or college graduates. The Word of God needs to be taught in the same way as it was written. This is why we should and must study the Scriptures sincerely, diligently, and daily. This is why the apostle Paul wrote in 2 Timothy 2:15, "**Study to shew thyself approved unto God, a workman that needeth not to be ashamed, rightly dividing the word of truth.**"

When done differently, certain truths and facts are never seen or experienced. The correct, loving, and true meanings of God become lost to His children. The ability to truly see God and His love becomes dim and dark, and not as bright as it should be. People become less likely to see God as He is. This of course discourages many and can harm God's children in many ways. Teaching the Scriptures without knowledge of our Lord has caused many, many problems over the centuries. Satan and his followers know this and encourage it. However, we need to know it as well, which should motivate us to dig deeper into God's Word and love, as often as we can.

There is another reason why certain facts and ideas are not brought out into the open, and that is because of the evil forces. We should all know by now, Satan and his followers do not want the truth to come out either, because it would hurt their ministry. Therefore, the world and its leaders have done and are doing their best to hide the true facts about God and His Word. They know it will harm them and their ministry if people learn the truth.

Still, I wondered why certain facts of the Scriptures have never been brought out into the light. Why were things hidden? Why are they still hidden in our translations today? Why did the Christians not do more in revealing the truth? Why did they go along with the status quo?

In the past, the more I thought and pondered about this fact, the more I came to believe there are many things in the Scriptures that are not meant for humankind to know at certain times. Or is it that humanity cannot fully understand God or want to understand Him?

Or, as we see often, humans have ways of diluting anything they place their hands on. And that especially includes the Word of God. We may never fully know (except when we leave this world) why our Lord allowed those translations to be used. But He knows.

Take, for instance, the names of God. Elohim, the all-powerful creators. El Shaddai, the All-powerful Provider of Life (women's breasts). God, the supreme being. Lord, overseer. LORD, God's personal name, YHWH, Yahweh.

When certain words are pronounced in the correct way and used in the correct way in the Scriptures, they change the meaning of their context. They bring out a completely different outlook on God and His Word. They enrich our minds and hearts to our great Creator. They bring us a little closer to Him. They shine a brighter light on God's love for humanity.

There are many words in our Scriptures that do not present their true meaning and in fact misrepresent what is being actually said. Take the translation for the word *love*. Most of the time, we take it as there is only one way or kind of love, but in the Holy Scriptures, there are three types: brotherly, godly, and marriageable.

Look at the words *forever, everlasting,* and *eternal.* Although they seem to be synonyms, when we look at these three words in their contexts, we will find that they do not have the same meaning. We usually use these words loosely as having the same meaning. But even our dictionary definitions for these words today are different. Look them up. And there are several words for hell (*hades, Sheol, Gehenna, Tartarus, Pit*). And the list goes on and on. And we will look a little more closely at the word *hell* in this book.

In this book, I will address many questions about what happens to us after we die. I will try to shed some light on the misconceptions and ideas that many may have and claim.

I will provide Scriptures from the King James Bible to back up what I believe are the true facts. All *italicized words* in those quotations represent my own added emphasis.

Now, before I go much further, I would say, I do not want to discredit any person for their ideas about hell and its ending, but I want to prove from God's own words what I believe to be true.

Many years ago, in 1974, God gave me a taste of hell in a way that I could understand, and I was horrified beyond belief. I know others have had various kinds of experiences of hell, and I am not saying they are wrong. Each person is unique, and God deals with each person in such a way that they can understand things.

But read this book with prayer and an open mind, and see where God leads you. And I believe that, at the end of this book, you will be praising our God Almighty even more. But do not take my word for it; search the Scriptures yourselves, and see what you find. Do not just take someone's word on it. Search for it *yourself.* Prove it yourself, as the apostle Paul tells us in 2 Timothy.

Chapter 1

My Hell Experience

This was an experience I had back in October 1974 in Baumholder, Germany. I was in the army and had transferred to a field artillery battalion. Back in those early years of my life, I was using some drugs, which I am not proud of today. At that time, I was not a Christian. I was doing what they call "my own thing."

I had only been in Germany for a few days and had gotten together with a group that also used drugs. They had taken me on a weekend camping trip in a castle near our post. They had gotten ahold of some hash, which I thought was extraordinarily strong, and I did not like it very much. I told these friends of mine about it and said I enjoyed doing acid or LSD more (what we considered hard drugs at that time besides heroin or speed). So one of them went out and got some purple microdot, which was how single hits of acid were sometimes supplied.

It was a Saturday evening, so we decided to take a hit of purple microdot. It was somewhere about five or six o'clock. Each of us took one, and it was beginning to get dark. Now, to me, the purple microdot was not very powerful at all, as I was used to taking four-way hits of windowpane or white blotter LSD, which was four times stronger than this one-way hit. But that evening, God had something else in mind for me. Not long after taking this hit, God placed me under His full and complete control.

Now, because of what I am going to tell you, you may believe the acid caused all of this. But that is far from the truth. Not long after I had taken the hit, I became incapacitated and was not aware of where I was or what I was doing. When this occurred, I asked my friends to put me in my room at the barracks (or sleeping quarters, as many would say) so I would not make a spectacle of myself or get into any trouble. When I was placed in the room, God immediately took absolute control, especially when I lay down on my army bunk. In the blink of an eye, I was placed at His disposal and could do nothing on my own.

He took me out of the realm of life in this world and placed me in an area that was unlike anything I had ever experienced or could explain. I had no idea where I was. I did not know whether it was heaven or not, but I knew God had me; He was in full control, and I had none whatsoever. I could not tell you if I was placed in a vision or in an actual place. But I knew it was real and not some figment of my imagination. He was in control. He placed me in what I considered an exceedingly small room or area that, to me, was indescribable.

I was all alone; nobody and nothing was there except me. It was a place of no sensory input whatsoever. I had all my senses, but there was nothing I could sense. I could smell, but there was nothing I could smell. I could taste, but there was nothing I could taste. I could see, but there was nothing I could see (not even a little color or black and white). I could hear, but there was nothing I could hear. I could feel, but there was nothing I could feel. The only thing I had and used was my memory.

My memories surrounded me like a Ferris wheel. They were all around me, and I could focus on them at any time, with no interruptions whatsoever.

Now, think about it: what would you do if you were incarcerated in that kind of place? What could you do? It was a place of waiting. A place of loneliness and waiting. But waiting for what? What would come to your mind? You would more than likely have the same thought I had. It was a place of waiting for judgment—what I, and probably you, would call "hell."

I was alone. There was nobody else. There was nothing else there besides me. There were no doors or windows.

There were not any physical flames, as many claim there are in hell. But my soul was on fire. What kind of fire, you may ask? A mental fire. An anxiety type of fire. Some of you may know what that feels like. This type of fire to me was horrible and beyond understanding.

There were no crowds or gatherings of people. Only me and my memories of my life experiences.

This was a place where the personal sins of my memories were brought out into the light of my mind. My mind alone, with no interruption from anything else or anyone else.

One could describe it as a place where the reflections of my life, while living in a sinful world, were brought out into the openness of my mind, to see as I had never seen them before, without any kind of interruption whatsoever. They were my life's personal inputs, sins, and thoughts, and they were only for me and God to view.

My friends, regardless of whether we like it or not, our sins are personal in nature to God, and they are only between each of us and Him. When our judgment comes, He will treat us as such and act on us as such—not as groups of people but as individuals. Since our sins are personal to God, hell will be personal for everyone. Everyone will answer for their own sins, regardless of what kind they are, how serious they may be, who caused them to sin, or how the sins were carried out. Regardless of whether we carried them out with others, we will answer for them individually.

But anyway, I knew, without any doubt whatsoever, that I had been placed in this holding area and was waiting for God's judgment. It was my waiting area to come before the Creator of the universe, and I knew without any kind of doubt I was very sinful and unclean. I knew I would be doomed when I met the almighty Judge and would have no excuse to stand on. I was guilty of violating God's laws and love. I was guilty of living in sinful ways, and I deserved His punishment. I was guilty of rejecting His offer of salvation.

What would you do if you were placed in this kind of situation? What could anyone do? It was a place of no sensory input whatsoever.

However, as I mentioned before, I did have my memory and personal thoughts. I began to relive my life over and over in my mind and see what I had done in the past and what I could have done to change my situation. All along, I knew I could not do anything. More than once I had reached a point in my life where I could have given my life to Christ, and then I would recall that I had not. Then the thought would come to me that this was hell, and there was nothing I could do. Then, suddenly, the Ferris wheel of my life would start over again in my mind.

It seemed like I was inside a Ferris wheel of my life, repeatedly watching my life experiences and story in bits and pieces going all around me. All along, I knew I was guilty and destined to be punished. I knew I was doomed and would be sentenced for my sins and discretions to the lake of fire when I met my Maker and Judge. I knew that the worst part of that would be meeting my Maker with great shame and embarrassment. That would set the stage to relive my life repeatedly, with no kind of interruptions whatsoever, and come to the same point in life repeatedly.

How many times had this happened? I had no idea, but it seemed to last a lifetime. Even though it seemed to take forever, it only actually took from two to four hours that night. Finally, somewhere around two or three o'clock in the morning, I exited that part of the vision or whatever it was. I went into a room with an angel sitting by a large door, guarding it. In his hands was a large book, and he was taking notes of everything.

Why he was taking notes, I did not know. Why he was guarding the door, I did not know. Why I was placed there, I did not know. But I was glad I was not in the Ferris wheel of my life anymore. I was not reliving my sinful past repeatedly.

After the shock wore off from having left a place of horror and entered another place, I asked this angel, "Why are you taking notes? What are you writing?"

He simply said, "I just am."

4

"Are you writing about me?"

He gave me no answer.

"Are you one of God's angels?"

Again, he gave me no answer.

"Why are you guarding this door?"

Again, he gave no answer.

"Why are you here?"

Again, no answer.

"What is on the other side of that door?"

Then he looked at me and asked, "What do you want it to be?"

It seemed as though I asked him these questions several times, and he gave me the same answers. Finally, I asked, "Is it heaven or hell on the other side of the door?"

He answered, "What do you want it to be?"

"Well," I said, "I sure do not want it to be hell, where I was just at."

I hoped he would say it was not, but he did not say a single word.

It seemed like hours passed as I was talking and asking him all kinds of questions. But finally, I got the nerve up and opened the door and walked in.

You see, I was scared that it was the doorway back to the place I had just left, and no way did I want to go back there. Finally, I opened the door and went through, and when I did, I looked and behold thousands and thousands of men and women sitting in things that resembled beanbags. Why beanbags? I did not know, but they resembled beanbags. I guess one reason was that back in that time, beanbags were popular, and you saw them everywhere. I did not care for them or like them personally. To me they were extremely uncomfortable. But anyway, there before me were thousands sitting in beanbags.

It took a while, but finally I entered this room, I looked and found one that was empty and sat down in it. When I did, my hand reached out and touched someone else, and suddenly, "I" or "me" did not exist anymore.

It was "we," no more "me," no more Jim, and we suddenly

5

turned into something that was around, red, warm, and staticky, what I would guess was a ball of energy. When this happened, the energy drew inward and then repeatedly expanded with a powerful force. As this was occurring, we began to ask ourselves, *What is this? Why is this happening to us? What is going on?* It seems that this energy was drawing inward and expanding with greater force each time it did happen, but why was it doing so? What was going on?

It seemed to last fifteen or twenty minutes. Then finally, at the peak, it began to explode, and we cried out, "This is the end." Then I came out of the vision or place, came to myself, and became fully aware of where I was. I was back in my barracks room and was what we often call "scared to death" and speechless. It was somewhere around five o'clock in the morning.

I thanked God I was still alive and was not in the Ferris wheel of life anymore. I was alive and tickled to make it through this obstacle (whatever it was). It was hell, the worst misery I had ever experienced.

Like that old country saying, "I had a relief, that you wouldn't believe," but at the same time, I also had a dread that you could not imagine either. I was relieved that this whole thing was finally over, and I was still alive. I was wondering to myself what had just happened. What was the reasoning behind it? I had never experienced anything like this, ever. I was frightened beyond measure. Was God showing me something, and was God trying to teach me something to learn about my life, in general? Why did I have to experience what I went through? What was I to learn from all of this?

I knew, without any doubt, that God had taken me through this whole thing to wake me up and turn me around in my life. But wake me up for what?

I began to recollect what I had just gone through. Exhausted, I walked over to my bunk and sat down to get some rest and maybe get some sleep, but I very quickly noticed that my mattress was soaking wet.

Why was my bed wet? I looked at it for a few moments and thought, did someone throw a bucket of water on it as a joke or prank? Did someone take a water hose and spray it down? But I knew nobody had been in this room but me. What was happening to me? How could my bed be wet? I knew it was dry when I took it as my bunk and laid in it earlier, but why was it wet now? *What is happening?*

Next, I thought, *Well, maybe I have wet the bed somehow, and now I am in a lot of trouble.* You see, in the Army, you could get a dishonorable discharge for wetting the bed, so I very quickly turned over the mattress. As I did, I noticed the other side was wet too. Sloppy wet, just like the other side.

Now, this disturbed and puzzled me. It would take a lot of water to soak an army mattress all the way through. How could something like this happen? I knew it was dry when I went into the room before all this happened. Again, I wondered if someone was pulling a prank on me, and if so, when did it happen? And if so, why?

I stood there looking and meditating on it for a while when I noticed the wetness on the mattress was also in the shape of a body. And it was all the way through the mattress, in the shape of a body, as if it were lying down. If someone were pulling a joke or prank on me, it would take some time to do this, and someone would have been noticed and seen doing it. And why the shape of a body? After giving this a lot of thought, I concluded that this had to be the hand of God. So, I grabbed a mattress from another bunk and placed it on my bed. Then, exhausted that this whole thing was finally over, I lay down and slept until noon that day.

For months, I pondered and wondered what all of that meant. I was in so much torment and pain in the Ferris wheel of life that I literally sweated unbelievably while in this vision or place. To me, there was no pain or torture that could match what I went through that night.

The memory of this was so horrible that it would not leave me. The thought of it frightened me daily. I could not get it out of my mind. It bothered me greatly that I could not get this out of my mind.

After this, for months, I was very afraid of going to sleep. You see, quite often, about the time I felt I was entering into the sleep cycle, I would feel like I was drifting off in that place again (the Ferris wheel of hell), and I would begin to sweat, and it would scare the living daylights out of me again.

There were many nights that I could not sleep at all. I was afraid that I would drift back into that hell again. And by no means did I want that. I never wanted to experience that ever again. To get any kind of sleep, I would go out and get drunk to help me go to sleep in any kind of way. I was tormented by the thought of experiencing that again.

Then one Sunday, about seven months later, in May, a close friend invited me to go to church with him. During the services, the message and Scripture reading began to stir my soul. I could not quite understand them, but they intrigued me deeply.

As I was leaving, on the way out, in the hallway, when I shook the preacher's hand, I told him I enjoyed the message, but could he explain more to me what he meant. I just did not get the message. Many were leaving at that time, and he was very busy with everyone leaving, so he grabbed a deacon as he was passing by, and asked him to explain the message and Scripture to me. Before I knew it, I had given my life over to Jesus.

After this, all the fear went away, and I became a new person on the inside. The thought of hell did not frighten me anymore. Then, I began to wonder if this vision was God's way of waking me up to turn my life around—to show me I needed a Savior to keep me from entering the pits of hell. I felt free, free from all troubles and worries from my life in the past. Free from the trouble and worries of living each day. Free from having to worry about going to hell. Even though I still had problems in life, I felt free. My problems did not matter much anymore.

But there was still a question as to why He had to be so harsh with me, that night when I experienced the Ferris wheel of hell. Was I so hardheaded that it had to take something like that to wake me up? Why did he have to place me literally in hell to get my attention?

And was there something else He wanted me to learn from this experience? Did it or should it have a special meaning to me, and if so, what? Why did I have to go through all of that?

I would not wish this on anyone unless—well, maybe unless it would allow them to accept Jesus, as I did that day in May. But the question is, did this vision or place have more for me than just waking me up to the fact that I needed a Savior and King?

For years, I believed it was just God's way of waking me up. God's way of showing me what hell is and will be like. But was there more? Is there another reason and explanation behind this miserable and painful experience?

Many would claim that it was the side effects of the drugs, but I know better. For instance, the bed being wet in the shape of my body was not caused by any kind of drugs I was taking. That is totally impossible. No person can sweat enough to sock a mattress or urinate enough to soak a mattress that way, regardless of what kind of drugs they are taking. There is not enough moisture in the human body to do that. It would kill a person to take out of their body that much water.

An army mattress was five or six inches in thickness. I do not know how much water is in a normal body, but I do know it had to take several gallons of water to soak an army mattress all the way through.

It would take God's intervention to make a person expel that much water from their body without killing them. Without God's intervention, there is no way this could have happened. That night, it was God working on me, not the drugs. What I did not know was that He was teaching me what happens after life for sinners without Jesus Christ.

Now, back then, I had taken acid or LSD so many times that I knew how they acted and responded to the body. I knew how long they lasted as well. For me, LSD four times as strong as what I took that night would only last between four to six hours at most. But this experience lasted nine to eleven hours, and I never received any kind of high on the drug that night.

For years, I pondered on the part of this vision or experience I had in hell, never giving much thought to the second part of it, being in the room with the angel and the door. To me, that room was the greatest relief from any kind of pain that I could have ever received. You could say it was life itself. A room where I left the place of torture and pain and went into a place of peace and quietness of the soul. A place of thought. A place of stillness. A place of reflections. A place of questions instead of a place of torments and regrets.

But after many years, I came to realize it was not only a place of peace, rest, and quietness of the soul, but the calm between hell and what is waiting. A waiting area for judgment.

You may think there is no way there can be a calm between hell and what is coming. But there is. You will find this in Revelation 20:11–13, which tells us there is:

> **And I saw a Great White Throne, and Him that sat on it, from whose face the earth and the heaven fled away; and there was found no place for them.**
>
> **And I saw the dead, small and great, stand before God; and the books were opened: and another book was opened, which is the book of life: and the dead were judged out of things which were written in the books, according to their works.**
>
> **And the sea gave up the dead which were in it; and death and hell delivered up the dead which were in them: and they were judged every man according to their works.**

It did not make sense to me that night that the angel in the waiting room was describing and showing me that there would be judgment and justice for all humankind. He was showing me that no one is exempt from judgment. All sinners will be judged according to their works, and all sinners without salvation from God will be found guilty.

My friends, every sinner will face their sins and rejection of Christ before their God. Everyone will be judged for their works and actions in this lifetime, and it is called the Great White Throne Judgment and the judgment of all sinners without Jesus.

This whole thing did not make sense to me until one day in the year 1996. At that point in my life, my wife and I had just moved into our new home.

One evening, around three or four o'clock, I was checking out the television stations and channels we had at this new location. As I switched to one channel, there was a preacher on, and he was preaching and teaching about the length of hell and its end. I became curious and began to watch.

He was saying that hell has an ending and will one day be "*no more.*" As I sat there watching and listening to him, being a preacher as well, I thought, *That cannot be true. That cannot be right*—even though I liked the thought. I myself have always preached that hell is eternal, and it cannot have an ending. The Bible says it is eternal.

But as he went on and explained many parts of the Scripture, which explains that hell has an ending, I became intrigued and interested in his message.

He ended his message with a challenge. He challenged everyone who was watching him, by saying: "Do not rely on my word, but search the Scriptures, and see for yourselves. Look up certain Scriptures, and see why they contradict themselves concerning hell."

Why does one verse say *everlasting* or *forever,* and others say *eternal*? Why do some Scriptures say *perish* and others do not? Why do certain Scriptures say *the destruction of the soul*?

Look at the whole Bible, not just the New Testament. Look into the Old Testament. Be in prayer, and keep an open head. Do not take my word or the word of others, but that of the living Word of God. See what it tells you. Pray and search.

So for weeks and months I did just that. I searched and re-searched the Scriptures almost every day, trying with an open mind to prove him wrong or right. Hoping that maybe he was right, but all along thinking he was wrong.

As days became weeks and weeks, months, I too concluded that he was right and that I had been wrong for years. And then, I realized that the conclusion of the vision that God gave me back in 1975 was a way of opening my eyes and mind to the fact that hell did have an ending, when I went into that room with all the thousands of people and sat down on something that looked like a beanbag and became that ball of energy and exploded. It was God's way of showing me the ending of hell in a way I could understand: the Lake of Fire. By this, I was shown that sinners will one day cease to be.

Those in hell right now will have an end. Their horrors, troubles, pains, agonies, and sufferings in the pit of hell, will one day cease. Until then, the horrors of will be like what is said in Psalm 115:4–7:

> **Their idols are silver and gold, the work of men's hands.**
> **They have mouths, but they speak not: eyes have they, but they see not.**
> **They have ears, but they hear not: noses have they, but they smell not.**
> **They have hands, but they handle not: feet have they, but they walk not: neither speak they through their throats.**

Just like worldly idols, those who choose to go to hell will resemble them, while in hell.

However, they will have an end to their miseries in hell. Not only will their pains and troubles end, but they will themselves. They will be annihilated from existence and from God.

I questioned myself as to why I had not seen this before. When I did, I could not help but start to praise God with my whole being.

Not only does our Lord provide men and women with a way to happiness and joy and being in His presence, but His love does not stop there. It goes on and on. His love for humanity cannot be described. It is beyond measure in every way. His love is beyond our comprehension in every way. Like many claims, "It is mind-blowing."

I have heard many say over the years that "God cannot be all love if He can watch those in hell suffer for eternity. That would take a heart of stone that has no love, to do that." But my friends, this is not the case.

As Christians, we all know God does not send anyone to hell. He gives and provides a way for everyone to escape the horrors of hell. And the "Way" is Jesus Christ. And still, His love goes on.

As Christians, we should all know that if we die and end up in the pits of hell, it will be our choice, not His. It is and will be our decision, not God's. It is not for any lack of love on God's part, but on ours. He wants no one to enter the door of hell. He wishes no one to perish.

But *if* we choose to enter those horrors, God will not intervene. However, as I am going to prove by the Scriptures, hell is not eternal, as many claimed. Yes, it is *forever* or *evermore*, but it is not *eternal*.

These are different words with different meanings. Regardless of what many believe, *forever* and *evermore* end with the end of "time," while eternity goes beyond time.

Now, when is the end of time? We find that mentioned in Revelation 20:11–15. The Lake of Fire is the end of everything evil and worldly.

Chapter 2

The Lake of Fire

What does the Bible say about the ending of hell? What do the Scriptures say about that? All my life, I have been taught that hell is eternal, and it has no ending.

Almost every denomination upholds this idea. However, many never mention this in their belief as a denomination with the Scriptures. If they do, it is with very few references. Hell has no ending; it exists in eternality and is final. They claim hell is eternal, believe and forget about it. Believe it and accept it as fact. There is no need to research eternal hell, because hell is eternal. No two ways about it. That is what the Scriptures teach, and that is final. No need to research anything different.

Personally, I had never had any reason to research it myself. That was what I was taught when I first became a Christian and what I believed for many years. For many years, I even taught and preached that myself. But there was always something in the back of my mind that bothered me about that fact. Something that just did not seem completely right about hell being eternity.

I could never put my finger on it, but something just did not fit right, until one day, as I mentioned in the previous chapter, I had moved to another location and turned the television on to check out the channels, when I stumbled across a channel where a preacher was preaching. And he was preaching something different than what I have been told over my years of life.

What kind of denomination this preacher was, I had no idea. But he was preaching a message about the end of hell and how the Holy Scriptures back this up in many places—not in a few verses of the Scripture, but throughout the whole Bible, from the beginning to the end.

He started with a few verses in Revelation and then went through the Bible, beginning from Genesis to Revelation. He mentioned verses that I had read and studied many times over the years. But he brought out the correct translations of certain words in those verses, which I have never heard or taught or even investigated before. And it amazed me greatly. They literally shocked and amazed me at the same time.

I wondered, How had I never connected these verses in God's holy Word with their real meaning? How many times have I preached on these verses of the Scriptures and missed their meaning? How could I be so blinded by tradition that has been passed down through the ages?

Why was his preaching moving my soul? Why was I so interested in his message? Was it God's way of waking me up to search His Word more deeply? Why was it digging into my heart? But I was moved deeply within to find out.

One of the first Scriptures he mentioned to prove this fact was Revelation 20:11, 13–15. So let us go to this Scripture.

> **And I saw the dead, small and great, stand before God; and the books were opened, which is the book of life: and the dead were judged out of those things which were written in the books, according to their works. [...]**
>
> **And the sea gave up the dead which were in it, and death and hell delivered up the dead where in them: and they were judged every man according to their works.**
>
> **And death and hell were cast into the lake of fire. This is the second death.**

And whosoever was not found written in the book of life was cast into the lake of fire.

Here we see something completely different from what most of us were taught in Sunday school or even in many sermons we have heard over the years. Here we find the "Lake of Fire."

Now, exactly what is the Lake of Fire? Is it another word for hell? Is it a continuation of hell? How can it be, when He says death and hell shall be cast into it? How can the Lake of Fire be explained?

Are the Scriptures contradicting themselves here? Are the translators of the Scriptures right or wrong when it comes to the Lake of Fire? Is it a continuation of hell, or is it literally a consuming type of fire?

What does God want us to learn and take to heart when it comes to the Lake of Fire? Which is it? A continuation of hell or a destructive type of fire?

What do you think? What exactly is the Lake of Fire? Is it a different type of hell, as many claimed? Is it a hotter fire? An advanced type? Or something completely different? What exactly is it? Which one is it?

This is the "Lake of Fire." However, many verses in the Scriptures explain it as a destructive or annihilating type of fire.

To understand this better, let us look at the word *fire*.

What is its meaning? What is associated with fire?

Living on this earth, we associate the word *fire* with destruction. Destroying, consuming, doing away with, ceases, ends.

What happens when fire consumes something? It destroys it and brings it to an end, or it ceases to be. It annihilates. Does fire last forever and forever? *No!*

Living on earth, we know fire goes out after the fuel and air are all consumed. When the substance feeding the fire is gone, the fire goes out. Take either one away, and the fire goes out.

After an object is destroyed or consumed by fire, it goes out and ends and leaves ashes. It does not keep on burning.

It ends or ceases to be. It destroys and consumes the object it is burning.

When the object is consumed, the fire goes out and leaves ashes. This is our way of thinking about the word *fire*.

And this is God's way of getting us to learn the truth about the Lake of Fire in Revelation. It is a destructive type of fire. But do not stop here in Revelation. Let us go to other parts of Scripture.

Another question that may arise here is whether the Lake of Fire and Brimstone are the same as the Lake of Fire. Revelation 20:10 reads: "**The devil, who deceived them, was cast into the lake of fire and brimstone where the beast and the false prophet are. And they will be tormented day and night forever and ever.**" Revelation 20:14 says, "**And anyone not found written in the Book of Life was cast into the lake of fire.**"

Are these separate places, or are they the same? Or does the "tormented day and night" deal with the time before the annihilation? I know, if I knew I would be destroyed, it would be torture to me, just thinking about it.

Verse 10 seems to indicate a place where time is still allowed, while verse 14 does not. But remember, time as we know ceases to be at the Great White Throne Judgment. After this, everything is made new, as mentioned in Revelation 21:1:, **Now I saw a new heaven and a new earth, for the first heaven and the first earth had *passed away.***" This passage insinuates that everything in the past is done away with, is no more. Nothing exists in the past after this takes place. Everything from this point is new.

Now let us examine some Scriptures from the Psalms and Proverbs:

> **But thou, O God, shalt bring them down into the pit of *destruction*: bloody and deceitful men shall not live out half their days.** (Psalm 55:23)

> **Surely, thou didst set them in slippery places: thou cast them down in *destruction*. How are**

they brought into desolation, as in a moment!
They are utterly consumed **with** *terrors.* (Psalm 73:18)

Shall thy lovingkindness be declared in the grave? Or thy faithfulness in *destruction*? (Psalm 88:11)

Who redeemed thy life from *destruction*, **who crowned thee with lovingkindness and tenders' mercies.** (Psalm 103:4)

The LORD preserved all of them that love Him: but all the wicked will he *destroys.* (Psalm 145:20)

The way of the LORD is strength to the upright: but *destruction* **shall be to the workers of iniquity.** (Proverbs 10:29)

Hell, and *destruction* **are before the LORD: how much more than the hearts of the children of men.** (Proverbs 15:11)

In these verses, we see the differences between the words *hell* and *destruction* and see that they indicate two separate events. Hell deals with torment and punishment, while destruction deals with ending things.

He loves transgression that loves strife: and he that exalts his gate seeks *destruction.* (Proverbs 17:19)

The Hebrew word here for destruction is *shamad*, which means to annihilate, perish, and destroy completely. To end, to cease to be. Not one that endures. Not one that goes on and on, on and on. It has an end.

> **It is joy to the just to do judgment: but** *destruction*
> **shall be to the workers of iniquity.** (Proverbs 21:15)

To whom? Sinners, workers of iniquity. Those who refuse to accept God's mercy and love. Those who refuse to accept His grace and forgiveness. Again, the word destruction is *shamad*. To end, to cease to be.

Now, let us go to Daniel and Malachi.

> **But the judgement shall sit, and they shall take**
> **away his dominion, to** *consume and to destroy* **it**
> **unto the end.** (Daniel 7:26)

> **For behold the day cometh that shall burn as**
> **an oven; that do wickedly, shall be stubble; and**
> **the day cometh shall** *burn* **them up, said the**
> **LORD of hosts, that it shall** *leave them neither* **root**
> **nor branch.** (Malachi 4:1)

Again, what exactly is the Lake of Fire? Is it not another word for hell, which lasts for eternity? It is consuming, it is destructive, and it ends. Regardless of whether we like it or not, it completely ends objects and annihilates them.

Now, what exactly happens to the souls there? They are burned up completely, as stated in Hebrews 6:8. They are annihilated. Hebrews 6:8 states, **"But that which bear thrones and briers is rejected and is nigh unto cursing; whose end is to be** *burned.***"** It is completely and entirely done away with. Punishment exists in hell, not in complete destruction.

In 1 Corinthians 10, we are told why Sodom and Gomorrah were destroyed. And why is it given in the Scriptures for us to learn? What is so important about the destruction of Sodom and Gomorrah? Why is it so important to teach us that it was destroyed? It did not say they were tormented and punished but destroyed. They are examples of what comes at the very end, by the Lake of Fire.

Now all these things happen unto them for *ensample*: and they are written for our admonition, upon whom the ends of the world are come. (1 Corinthians 10:11)

Even as Sodom and Gomorrah, and the cities about them in like manner, giving themselves over to fornication, and going after strange flesh, are set forth for an *example*, suffering the vengeance of eternal fire. (Jude 7)

It was for humankind to learn their fate themselves for rejecting their Lord and Savior and to learn what lies ahead for the existence of humans, if they fail to accept our God's salvation. It is for those who reject Jesus's sacrifice—those who willingly neglect God's grace and accept their own salvational plan; those who are lovers of self, rather than those who listen to Jehovah (the Supreme Being). Sodom and Gomorrah were places of such people. They were like those we see today in a lot of our societies. The did their own thing, regardless of the consequences they may face. They only looked for the here and now and made no plans for later. Because of their attitude toward life, God destroyed them. God sent them to hell at their death, but He destroyed their cities.

Now remember, Sodom and Gomorrah were *completely destroyed*. They were annihilated, not tormented and tortured. God completely ended their reign and destroyed their cities. They ceased to be.

Therefore, this implies that the Lake of Fire is a consuming fire, a destructive type of fire, which indicates an end of all souls of those who fail to give themselves to the mercy of our Lord God.

The Lake of Fire has no punishments and horrors that we associate with hell. The Lake of Fire is the last fate for fallen humankind and the coming judgment for all who do not receive God's salvation, and it will be the end of their existence (eternally). Meaning they will never live again in any shape, form, or fashion.

Again, the Great White Throne Judgment, the Lake of Fire, is a consuming, ending type of fire or destruction. Not one that endures but one that has an ending.

Another question may arise here as you read these Scriptures concerning destruction. Where is the torment and torture? Sodom and Gomorrah were not tormented and tortured but were *completely destroyed*. They came to an end. No torment and torture are mentioned when we find destruction in the Scriptures. Why is it?

One reason is that destruction and hell are two different realities. They are not the same, as many would have you believe.

I believe that in one (hell), there is mention of weeping and gnashing of teeth before and while in it. In the other (the Lake of Fire), the misery happens before it takes place.

And turning the cities of Sodom and Gomorrah into ashes condemned them with an overthrow, making them an *ensample* unto those that after should live ungodly. (2 Peter 2:6)

Even as Sodom and Gomorrah, and the cities about them in like manner, giving themselves over to fornication, and going after strange flesh, are set forth for an *example*, suffering the vengeance of eternal fire. (Jude 7)

Again, as seen in these verses of Scripture, these cities were not punished or tormented. They were annihilated and destroyed. Their existence ended, and they ceased to be.

Therefore, these verses imply that the Lake of Fire, or eternal fire, is a destructive type of fire: not one that endures, but one that consumes completely. One that ends.

Hell is a place of condemnation. What is the definition of condemnation? Webster's definition of condemnation is a state of being condemned, convicted, sentenced, to doom, to declare convertible to public use under the right of eminent domain.

The Strongs Complete Dictionary of Bible Words says *katakrima* or *katakrisis* means decision (*krisis*), tribunal justice.

Condemn (*rasha*) means to declare wrong, (*katakaio*) judge against, (*krino*) to punish.

Condemned (*rasha*) means declared wrong, (*katakrino*) judged against.

Condemnation is the process of being sentenced to a place for punishment. It means to sentence, to bring to justice, to set things right. Remember this when we read these next verses.

> **Verily, verily, I say unto you, he that heareth my word, and believeth on him that sent me, hath everlasting life, and shall not come into condemnation, but is passed from death into life.** (John 5:29)

> **There is therefore now no condemnation to them which are in Christ Jesus, who walk not after the flesh, but after the Spirit.** (Romans 8:1)

What was Jesus talking about when He was mentioning condemnation? He was talking about the process of judging and punishing those who refuse His salvation.

Therefore, if our lives should end today and we have not accepted Jesus Christ as our Lord and Savior, we will again, like the old saying, split the doors wide open.

Both hell and the Lake of Fire *exist for those* who walk after the flesh. However, they are completely different in nature.

Many may feel and believe that if hell has an ending, they can do as they like and not pay the consequences or price. But that is not so.

There is a price to be paid for rejecting Christ and living the way of the world. And it is not very pleasant at all. And it is called hell, a place of condemnation (enduring torment and torture). Then, later, there comes the Lake of Fire at the Great White Throne Judgment (the complete destruction of the soul).

Both hell and the Lake of Fire are places of receiving just reward or punishment. We cannot just live like we desire and one day just disappear, or be consumed, or cease to be, as many today would have you to believe. As God's creation, there are consequences for the failure to receive His plans for our salvation.

Each person who refuses God's salvation will pay the price for their rejection in two ways: both hell and the Lake of Fire.

In these verses of John and Romans, Jesus is not only speaking about the second death at this certain time but the punishments of hell.

Therefore, we need to understand hell is not some kind of vacation between earth and judgment at the end (the Lake of Fire) and is not a place of rest and sleep, as many may claim.

Hell is a place of horror, agony, pain, and gnashing of teeth, a place where the worm dies not. It is not to be taken for granted or lightly. There will be justice for all who reject Christ as Lord.

Again, hell is not a place to be taken for granted. It is a real place, not some imaginary existence or fairy tale that many may claim and hold on to today. However, it is not eternal in nature.

We also need to remember Satan and his followers will one day be destroyed as well. They will not spend eternity in hell, as many claimed. You can find this mentioned in Ezekiel 28:14. He will spend some time there in hell, as mentioned in Revelation:

> **And I saw an angel come down from heaven, having the key of the bottomless pit and a great chain in his hand.**
>
> **And he laid hold on the dragon, that old serpent, which is the Devil, and Satan, and bound him a thousand years.**
>
> **And cast him into the bottomless pit, and shut him up, and set a seal upon him, that he should deceive the nations no more, till**

the thousand years should be fulfilled, and after that he must be loosed a little season. (Revelation 20:1–3)

But at the end of time, he and his followers will cease to be, as stated in Revelation 20:10 and Ezekiel, chapter 28. Let's look at Ezekiel 28.

Thou art the anointed cherub that covereth; and I have set thee; thou wast upon the holy mountain of God; thou hast walked up and down in the midst of the stones of fire.

Thou wast perfect in thy ways from the day that thou wast created, till iniquity was found in thee.

By the multitude of thy merchandise they have filled the midst of thee with violence, and thou hast sinned: therefore, I will cast thee as profane out of the mountain of God; I will *destroy thee*, O covering cherub, from the midst of the stones of fire.

Thine heart was lifted up because of thy beauty, thou hast corrupted thy wisdom by reason of thy brightness; I will cast thee to the ground, I will lay thee before kings, that they may behold thee.

Thou hast defiled thy sanctuaries by the multitude of thine iniquities, by the iniquity of thy traffick; therefore, will I bring forth a fire from the midst of thee, it shall *devour thee*, and I will *bring thee to ashes* upon the earth in the sight of all them that behold thee.

All they that know thee among the people shall be astonished at thee; thou shalt be a

terror, and *never shalt thou be anymore.* (Ezekiel 28:14–19)

By this Scripture in Ezekiel, we see and find that at the very end, Satan will be completely annihilated, consumed, destroyed, and reduced to ashes. He is not destined to spend eternity in hell but will be destroyed. Verse 16 says he will be destroyed. Verse 18 says he will "be devoured" and be "brought to ashes." Verse 19 says he will "never be anymore." Now, what does this tell us about the Lake of Fire and the kind of fire it is?

As we find in Revelation, Satan is cast into the Lake of Fire, to be destroyed, as mentioned in Ezekiel, and after that the rest of fallen humanity joins him. They will be no more. Nada, nothing. They will be annihilated, consumed, and destroyed, once and for all, throughout all eternity. Never to exist ever again in any kind of way.

Chapter 3

Everlasting and Eternal

In many verses of our Scripture, we will find the words "everlasting and eternal." For the most part, we usually believe these words have the same meaning. Again, if you do some research on these words, you will find something different.

Webster's dictionary and others define *everlasting* and *forever* as something that deals with *time*. As long as time exists, they exist. However, eternity goes beyond time itself.

As human beings, we deal with time. We like to think we can understand eternity. But the fact is, we cannot comprehend the idea of eternity. We may believe we can, but we cannot.

Our bodies are finite and built to exist in time as we know it. We live in time while we exist in our finite bodies. We live day by day, with each day having twenty-four hours, and each hour having sixty minutes, and each minute having sixty seconds.

Think about it.

We live in days and years, with 365 days a year, unless it is a leap year. We think in time, we live in time, and we exist in time, as we live in our finite bodies, while we are living on this finite earth.

Our every action and our every thought happens because of time. There is nothing we do while living in our finite bodies that does not deal with time. Therefore, *forever* or *everlasting* deals with our existence with time on planet Earth. Everything we do exists in time. We live in time, feel in time, and think in time. There is nothing we do that does not deal with time. However, one day, time will cease, and there will be an end to time as we know it.

Now, when will time end? When will the existence of time and earth's end occur?

As children of God, we should all know by now when they will end: at the Great White Throne Judgment and the Lake of Fire; at the end of existence as we know it. Death and hell will not end in time. Death and hell exist in time, like everything else in our lives.

Let me ask you this:

What is the first book every newborn Christian desires to read and study? Instead of Genesis, which is the Bible's first book and should be read first, we want to turn to Revelation and see how it ends.

Like most newborn Christians, I too turned to Revelation and read it first, raising a million questions. Many newborn Christians read and study Revelation, all along scratching their heads in confusion and asking many questions—and usually overlooking the end, overlooking the obvious, overlooking what is in plain sight in God's holy words. Never noticing the meaning of the end.

Everything we see, hear, feel, and smell deals with time and will all end one day in the future. Nothing we see, hear, feel, or smell will last long. They are not eternal. Our world and existence are always changing, decaying, and ending. It is a part of our life as we know it. Yes, even time itself will end. However, it all ends, and eternity will come into existence for every believer.

> **Wherefore if thy hand or thy foot offend thee, cut them off, and cast them from thee: it is better for thee to enter into life halt or maimed, rather than having two hands or two feet to be cast into everlasting fire.** (Matthew 18:8)

> **Then shall He say also unto them on the left hand, depart from me, ye cursed, into**

everlasting fire, prepared for the devil and his angels. (Matthew 25:41)

And these shall go away into everlasting punishment, but the righteous into *life eternal.* (Matthew 25:46)

Certain Scriptures themselves make it very plain, repeatedly, that heaven is eternal, while hell is everlasting. It also shows us very clearly that there is a difference between *everlasting* and *eternal*, as explained in the following verses.

The Greek word for "everlasting" at times will differ from what many believe. The Greek word for everlasting is *aion* or *aionios*, which means a span of time, a limited age. In other words, it deals with earthly or worldly time as we know it.

Matthew 25:41 says, **"Then shall he say also unto them on the left hand, depart from me, ye cursed, into everlasting fire, prepared for the devil and his angels."**

What shall I do to inherit eternal life? **"And a certain ruler asked Him, saying, good master, what shall I do to inherit eternal life?"** (Luke 18:18).

Eternal salvation: **"And being made perfect, he became the author of eternal salvation unto all of them that obey Him"** (Hebrews 5:9).

King eternal: **"Now unto the King eternal, invisible, the only wise God, be honor and glory forever and ever. Amen"** (1 Timothy 1:17).

Eternal in the heavens: **"For we know that if our eternal house of this tabernacle were dissolved, we have a building of God, a house not made with hands, eternal in the heavens"** (2 Corinthians 5:1).

Things which are not seen are eternal: **"While we look not at the things which are seen, but at the things which are seen, but at the things which are seen are temporal, but the things which are not seen are eternal"** (*2 Corinthians 4:18*).

His eternal glory by Christ Jesus: "**But the God of all grace, who hath called us unto his eternal glory by Christ Jesus, after that ye have suffered a while, make you perfect, establish, strengthen, settle you**" (1 Peter 5:10).

Chapter 4

Perish and Destruction

The word *perish* means the same as *annihilate*. The word *perish* in John 3:16 means to destroy, which is to annihilate.

As we have seen before, the Greek word translated "forever" is *aion, aionios*, which means time period or limited age.

Perishing and destroying do not mean enduring punishment, as many would have you believe.

There are other words we associate with annihilating, like to *do away with*, to *end*, and to *cease to be*, to annihilate, and to destroy.

What were the demons saying when they spoke to Jesus in Mark 1:24, "Saying, let us alone. What have we to do with thee, thou Jesus of Nazareth? Art, thou come to *destroy* us? I know thee who thou art, the Holy One of God."

> **And fear not them which kill the body but are not able to kill the soul: but rather fear Him which is able to *destroy* both body and soul.** (Matthew 10:28)

Here, the Scripture does not say to send body and soul to hell to be tortured and tormented. No! He said to *destroy*.

The Greek word here for destroy in this verse is *apollumi*, which means to destroy fully, to annihilate.

When the demonic man at the synagogue met Jesus, in Mark

1:23–24, "he cried out Let us alone: what have we to do with thee, thou Jesus of Nazareth? Art, thou come *to destroy us?*"

They did not say "send us to hell," did they?

> **Know ye not that ye are the temple of God, and that the Spirit of God dwelled in you? If any man defiles the temple of God, him shall God** *destroy*; **for the temple of God is holy, which temple are ye?** (1 Corinthians 3:16)

Again, He said, "destroy," not "send to hell."

> **Forasmuch then as the children are partakers of flesh and blood, he also himself likewise took part of the same: that though death he might** *destroy* **him that had the power of death, that is the devil.** (Hebrews 2:14

Again, the verse does not say to "send to hell."

Even though Satan will be sent to hell, here it is talking about the end judgment, at the Great White Throne. An annihilation type of judgment. One that ends and ceases to be.

The word *destroy* in the Scriptures is different from sending someone to hell for punishment, as many would have us believe.

In James 4:12, we read, **"There is one lawgiver who is able to save and** *destroy*: **who art thou that judges another."**

Regardless of what many may believe, there is a significant difference between sending to hell and destroying.

What does Jesus say about destruction?

> **Enter ye in at the strait gate; for wide is the gate and broad is the way, which leads to** *destruction*, **and many there be which go in there at**. (Matthew 7:13)

He is not saying send to hell, but the destruction of the soul. An ending of the soul. Not punishment.

But an ending.

Again, this does not mean taking away the punishment either. Romans 3:16 says, "**Destruction and Misery are in their ways.**" Whose ways? The wicked. Those who never accepted Christ as Lord and King. Again, the Scripture says destruction, not punishment or send to hell.

> **Whose end is** *destruction*, **whose God is their belly and whose glory is in their shame, who mind earthly things.** (Philippians 3:19)

What is their end? "*Destruction.*"

This verse does not say hell, does it?

The Hebrew word for destruction is *apoleia*, which means to perish, die, waste, and be destroyed—to cease to be, to be consumed.

> **For wickedness burns as the fire: it shall devour the briers and thorns and shall kindle in the thickets of the forest, and they shall mount up like the lifting up of smoke. Through the wrath of the Lord of hosts is the land darkened, and the people shall be as the fuel of the fire: no men shall spare his brother.** (Isaiah 9:18–19)

What do we associate *devour* with? Not torture and torment, but destruction and annihilation. An end.

> **As therefore the tares are gathered and** *burned* **in the fire; so, shall it be at the end of this world.**
> **The Son of man shall send forth his angels, and they shall gather out of his kingdom all things that offend, and them which do iniquity.**

And cast them into a furnace of fire; there shall be wailing and gnashing of teeth. (Matthew 13:40–42)

So shall it be at the end of the world; the angels shall come forth and sever the wicked from among the just.

And shall cast them into the furnace of fire; there shall be wailing and gnashing of teeth. (Matthew 13:49–50)

Hebrews 6:8 states, **"But that which bear thrones and briers is rejected and is nigh unto cursing; whose end is to be burned."**

If a man abides not in me, he is cast forth as a branch, and is withered; and men gather them, and cast them into the fire, and they *are burned*. (John 15:6)

Burning is a type of destruction. It destroys. It consumes. It ends. It annihilates.

Hold a lighted match under a piece of paper to see what happens. Fire will consume it or, in other words, annihilate it. It becomes ash and eventually disappears.

Ceases to be, doesn't it?

It cannot be put back together again.

We should all know that God can do all things, but when He burns something or casts it into fire, there is no existence for it ever again, period. It simply ceases to be, no longer exists.

But the transgressors shall be *destroyed together*: **the end of the wicked shall be cut off.** (Psalm 37:38)

34

The Hebrew word here is *shamad*, meaning to destroy, to perish. It does not mean to punish or to endure torment and pain. But comes to a complete ending. Again, cease to be.

Psalm 9:5–6 states, **"Thou has rebuked the heathen, thou have destroyed the wicked, thou have put out their name forever and ever. O thou, enemy, *destructions* are come to a perpetual end: and thou have destroyed cities; their memorial is *perished* with them."**

Now, what is said here? This Scripture does not say to send to hell, but to destroy.

The Hebrew word here is *abad*, which means to destroy or perish as well. In other words, this says the wicked (the lost, those who do not claim Jesus as Lord and Savior) will be destroyed.

The word *perpetual* means on and on and on and on. Never-ending, a complete ending.

Nothing comes back from being destroyed. Once destroyed, always destroyed.

We cannot bring a piece of paper or anything back after it is consumed with fire.

Again, I know God can do all things, but He is saying here they will never be brought back for any reason. Never to be restored again. Never to exist again.

Philippians 3:19 states that the sinner's end is *destruction*: **"Whose end is *destruction*, whose God is their belly, and whose glory is in their shame, who mind earthly things."**

Who shall be punished with everlasting *destruction* from the presence of the Lord and from the glory of his power. (2 Thessalonians 1:9)

The word for destruction here in Greek is *ollumi*, which means to destroy, to perish, to cease to be, to annihilate.

In one NIV Bible translation I have, at the bottom margin is a note stating that the word *destruction* in this verse of 2 Thessalonians does not mean annihilation, but send to hell. In other words, the word *destruction* is a generic word for hell, but he did not explain why. He gave no explanation as to why *destruction* is another word for hell. I question his explanation on this word, knowing all along others will not, and will believe because he wrote it in the Word of God, even though it was his explanation rather than God's words.

Why was *destruction* used instead of *hell* in this verse? Why did he not look up the original Greek word? He simply started to look up a couple more verses in Scripture that use this word in a generic form. When I did, it still did not explain his idea.

When I see information like this presented in our Scriptures today, I often wonder, where are they getting their facts from? Is it from their past experiences in the church, their education, or is it easier for them to believe it? Where did their knowledge come from?

I hope and pray I will never lead anyone astray from the true facts of the Scriptures. But I know many things in our society will do so. Therefore, I challenge everyone to research the Scriptures and everything they read that is speaking about God's words. Do not take anyone's word for it, especially mine.

Like everyone else, I know I make mistakes and errors. I will never be perfect while living in this world. (Please don't tell my wife that.) None of us will. That is the main reason we need to be always in prayer with our Great Creator.

We need to do what 2 Timothy 2:15 says: **"Study to shew thyself approved: a workman that needeth not to be ashamed, rightly dividing the word of truth."**

We need to always prove the Scripture in the right context. And never take any other word for it.

Prove them ourselves as 2 Timothy 4:2–5 states:

Preach the word; be instant in season, out of season; reprove, rebuke, exhort with all longsuffering and doctrine.

For the time will come when they will not endure sound doctrine; but after their own lusts

shall they heap to themselves teachers, having itching ears.

And they shall turn away their ears from the truth and shall be turned into fables.

But watch thou in all things, endure affliction, do the work of an evangelist, make full proof of thy ministry.

Study, search, and prove the Scriptures, and find the truth yourself. Forget what you have been told. Do not take anyone's word for it unless it is backed up with the Scriptures.

Over the years, I have heard things such as "Brother so-and-so said it, so it must be the absolute truth. Sister so-and-so said it, and she is always right." However, all of us are human beings, and as such, we all make mistakes. Only God and His Word are perfect in every way. Therefore, we have an obligation to God and ourselves to find the truth, especially about His perfect Word, which is life itself, something that should be held in high esteem by every child of God and not be taken for granted.

This is why I am writing this book. This is why I am bringing out into the open all these verses in Scripture for you to examine. Study them, pray, and see for yourselves if they are right or wrong. Again, do not take my word or any other person's word for it, but study the Scriptures yourself, and find and get the facts for yourselves. Study and pray.

There is another question I would like to ask everyone who reads this book, "What is more frightening, the thought of going to hell or the thought of being erased completely from existence?"—that is, being erased from our existence on earth and erased from God's existence altogether. If you think about it, both are quite scary. But which one is worse? Which one would haunt you the most? Which one would haunt you if you were an atheist? If you were on your deathbed, which one would scare you the most? Which one would create the most fear?

Today, many nonbelievers, or should I say lost sinners, believe that this life is all there is, and it is hard for them to contemplate the thought of death. Usually, at the deathbed, they climb the walls at the end of their lives, looking for anything to extend their human lives, anything to give them a little more time on this earth. Usually, it is the same for backslidden Christians, but it seems to be more so for those who are atheists. Why is it?

Why are many people today willing to try anything to live longer? What is so special about this worldly existence that many are willing to freeze themselves, or be placed into suspended animation, in order to live a little longer? Is it the thought of going to hell for their rejection of Christ, or is it the thought of ceasing to be, or perishing from existence? Which one is it? What do you think?

Chapter 5

Descriptions of Hell

The early Hebrews believed that the dead descend into some kind of immobile and inanimate existence in the netherworld (*Sheol, hades*).

The same fate awaits both the righteous and the wicked alike.

Later, hell was considered and identified with *Gehenna*, resulting in the concept of hell as a place of punishment for the wicked.

Rabbinic Judaism has no dogmatic formulations of this concept, which is still primarily one of folklore, with the most diverse views existing side by side.

Primarily, hell, in rabbinic Judaism, is a purgatory with a maximum stay of twelve months. Only certain classes of the very wicked were said to be permanently doomed to hell. In Christianity, hell is the *abode of Satan*, the fallen angels, and the damned.

According to the Apostles' Creed, Christ descended into hell prior to His resurrection, thereby saving from hell all those who accepted Him as their Christ and Lord of creation after His death and at this descent.

Modernistic forms of both Judaism and Christianity tend to *de-emphasize* the concept of hell, substituting for people's awareness of their distance from God after acts of wrongdoings.

In the Scripture, we find several depictions of hell: *Sheol, hades, the Pit, hell, Gehenna, Topheth, Tartarus,* and *the Abyss.*

The *Abyss* is a bottomless pit mentioned in Revelation 9:2 and is described as a special place where certain demons are held in chains.

Gehenna is a Latin word for the Hebrew term Valley of Hinnom (hell) along with *Topheth.*

Hades is a Greek word that is the same as *Sheol.*

Pit is sometimes equivalent to *Sheol.*

There are thirteen different words for Pit; again, a few of them mean *Sheol.*

Hades (Greek) and *Sheol* (Hebrew) are the different words for the same state of departed spirits.

In the ancient world in which the Bible originated, death was called the land of no return and was viewed as an inescapable underworld prison.

The OT pictures the realm of death (*Sheol*) as being under the earth, comparing its entrance to a deep pit. And it is considered the realm of the dead.

Tartarus is Greek for hell, found in 2 Peter 2:4, a place where the wicked angels are held for judgment. The Greeks taught that *Tartarus* was a place lower than *hades* and was reserved for the wickedest human beings, gods, and demons.

The Jews eventually came to use this term to describe the place where fallen angels were sent. To them, it was the lowest hell, the deepest pit, and the most terrible place of torture and eternal suffering.

Topheth, described in Isaiah 30:33, is used as the same word *Gehenna.*

What are some other descriptions of hell mentioned in the Scriptures?

Matthew 5:25 offers the description of a prison: "**Agree with thine adversary quickly, whiles thou art in the way with him; lest at any time the adversary deliver thee to judge, and the judge deliver thee to the officer, and thou be cast into prison.**"

Matthew 5:22 says it is a hell of fire: "**But I say unto you, that whosoever is angry with his brother without cause shall be in danger of judgment; and whosoever shall say to his brother,**"

Raca, shall be in danger of counsel; but whosoever shall say, thou fool, shall be in danger of hell fire."

Matthew 18:9 also says, "And if thine eye offends thee, pluck it out, and cast it from thee; it is better for thee to enter into life with one eye, rather than having two eyes to be cast into hell fire."

Mark 9:43 shows an unquenchable fire: "And if thy hand offends thee, cut it off; it is better for thee to enter into life maimed than having two hands to go into hell, into the fire that never shall be quenched."

Matthew 8:12 says it is outer darkness: "But the children of the kingdom shall be cast out into outer darkness; there shall be weeping and gnashing of teeth."

Mark 9:47–48 says it is a place where the worm does not die. "And if thine eye offend thee, pluck it out; it is better for thee to enter into the kingdom of God with one eye than having two eyes to be cast into hell fire. Where their worm dieth not, and the fire is not quenched."

What exactly is hell? Is hell a place where fire as we know it burns us constantly in pain as we know it today?

Do lost sinners burn constantly, with no relief, burning the flesh, causing blisters and all sorts of suffering in their bodies?

Will we have bodies as we have now? Or is it the suffering of our souls? Will our souls burn with a type of physical fire? No!

They will burn with a type of mental fire. A fire of the soul or mind. What kind of fire is that? Many of us would call it an anxiety multiplied many, many times in intensity.

Now, I would like to stop here and chase a rabbit, so to say. I always enjoyed doing that when I used to preach. The type of fire in hell is an "anxiety type" of fire. It consumes the soul or mind. Those of you who have ever had an anxiety attack will know what I am talking about. When a person has an anxiety attack, they begin to be overwhelmed with all their problems and all their situations in life. They begin to be overwhelmed with heat and other things, so that they begin to sweat. They cannot think and respond as they should. Life itself overwhelms them tremendously.

This is why many take their own lives during anxiety attacks. To them living in this world is useless and not worth it. They want to end it all. Life does not make sense and is harmful. Their minds are consumed with all kinds of things that do not make sense. Their bodies do not respond to their minds when anxiety hits. They feel like puppets in a world where they have no control whatsoever. controlled by something that they do not like.

Now, what kind of body did the rich man have? He did not have one. His soul was there, not his body, and it was his soul that was on fire. Therefore, he wanted anything to take his mind off his situation in hell. If his soul were on fire as a physical body, he would not be crying for a fire truck, a pond, or a lake to put him out of his misery, instead of one drop of water. By this, we see it will be a different type of burning in hell than what we see in the world we live in now. One that is much worse than what we can imagine here.

Is it a bottomless pit filled with brimstone, diesel, gas, propane, kerosene or anything else that will unite into a fervent heat? *No!* It is much, much worse. Those in hell would wish it were. Hellfire is a fire of the soul, not the body. It is a different kind of fire, not one as we know that destroys finite things or one at the very end.

Remember, our souls are not finite, as everything in this world is. Our souls were created to live beyond this world. Therefore, what exactly is the type of fire that exists in hell?

Most would consider agony, disturbance, and misery is a type of hell of the soul.

I do.

Hellfire is the burning of the soul, not our physical bodies. It is a different type of burning than anything we have experienced in our lives here on Earth.

But what kind of agony, disturbance, and misery would be considered hell?

It is an anxiety type, multiply several times. You may ask what is an *anxiety type of fire*? Webster's Dictionary for *anxiety* is "A painful or apprehensive of mind, an impending or anticipated ill. Fearful concern or interest. An abnormal and overwhelming sense of apprehension and fear often marked by physiological signs (as sweating, tensions, and increased pulse) of doubt concerning the reality and nature of the threat and by self-doubt about one's capacity to cope."

Also, the fact that a person is there to start with would be one type. The fact that they did not listen to God and His instructions is another. Not only did they allow themselves to be placed there, but they may also allow others they knew and loved to be placed there as well. They knew all along it was their own choice to escape hellfire, but they did not do anything about it while living. They knew they did not have to end up there, but they did.

Again, I believe hell is a place with no sensory input whatsoever, a place of loneliness, a place of remembrance and regrets with no way of escape. A place of incineration of the soul. Doesn't that sound like hell to you? Remember what Psalm 117:4–7 says:

Their idols are silver and gold, the work of men's hands.

They have mouths, but they speak not; eyes have they, but they see not.

They have ears, but they hear not; noses have they, but they smell not.

They have hands, but they handle not; feet have they, but they walk nor: neither speak through their throat.

Like the idols many used to worship, sinners in hell are incinerated in a place where they have all their senses but can use none of them. They are aware of where they are but can do nothing about it. To me the word *horrible* cannot describe hell sufficiently.

The Scriptures also describe hell as a place of gnashing of teeth as described in Matthew 8:12: "**But the children of the kingdom shall be cast out into outer darkness; there shall be weeping**

and gnashing of teeth." We find that also mentioned in Matthew 13:42; 24:51; and 25:30.

So what is "gnashing of teeth"?

I remember that, as a child, I would grit my teeth while sleeping whenever I would get sick. My mother told me that I could be heard a mile away. At that time in my life, I did not know I was gritting my teeth.

All I knew was I felt really bad and in a kind of distress and agony. I was miserable and hurting down on the inside. Therefore, I concluded that gritting my teeth was a type of release from my pain. And this will probably be true for those in hell.

The pains and agony of those in hell will be so horrible that gritting their teeth will be just one way of releasing a little of their suffering, as well as weeping. And weeping for what? Why weep or cry in hell?

Who will they be crying or weeping for besides themselves?

They will not only be weeping for themselves, because they ended up there, but for others they knew ended up there because of their actions or inactions during their lifetimes. The miseries they cause themselves and the misery they caused for others will obsess them.

Notice in Luke, the rich man wanted to have someone warn his brothers of his situation and pains in hell lest they should fall into the same place.

Hell is a place of the weeping of the soul. It is not only a place of regrets, but also a place where you are ashamed of being. A place of shame and regrets. A place of guilt and misery.

The Hebrew word for hell (*Gahanna* or *Geenna*) in some places *literally* means a place of *incineration*.

And we associate that with being in prison, locked up, and punished for what we did wrong.

You could say hell is a waiting area, filled with horrors and torment waiting for the judgment of Almighty God. A place of no escape. A place to anticipate one's final judgment.

The Greek word *Geenna* denotes a waiting place of *fiery punishment*.

Geenna is derived from the Hebrew Ge Hinnom, the valley of Hinnom (a gorge on the south side of Jerusalem).

It was at that gorge on the south side of Jerusalem that the Israelite people conducted the heathen rite of burning children to Molech, as told in 2 Chronicles 28:3.

Jeremiah predicted that because of this sin, the LORD would make the valley a *"Valley of Slaughter,"* where the corpses of the Israelites would be buried till there was no more place for them. The remaining bodies were to be food for the birds (Jeremiah 7:32–33).

Jeremiah's prophecy undoubtedly led Israel to view Ge Hinnom as a place of judgment of the wicked, a place of abhorrence, punishment, and shame. Later, rabbinical tradition considered it a place for burning carcasses and rubbish.

Moreover he burnt incense in the valley of the son of Hinnom, and burnt his children in the fire, after the abominations of the heathen whom the LORD had cast out before the children of Israel. (2 Chronicles 28:3)

Manasseh was twelve years old when he began to reign, and he reigned fifty and five years in Jerusalem.

But did that which was evil in the sight of the LORD, like unto the abominations of the heathen, whom the LORD had cast out before the children of Israel.

For he built again the high places which Hezekiah his father had broken down, and he reared up altars for Balaam, and made groves, and worshipped all the host of heavens, and served them.

Also, he built altars in the house of the LORD, whereof the LORD had said, In Jerusalem shall my name be forever.

> And he built altars for all the host of heaven in the two courts of the house of the LORD.
>
> And he caused his children to pass through the fire in the valley of the son of Hinnom; also, he observed times, and used enchantments, and dealt with a familiar spirit, and wizards; he wrought much evil in the sight of the LORD, to provoke him to anger. (2 Chronicles 33:1–6)
>
> Therefore, behold, the days come, saith the LORD, that it shall no more be called Tophet, nor the valley of the son of Hinnom, but the valley slaughter; for they shall bury in Tophet, till there be no place.
>
> And the carcasses of these people shall be meat for the fowls of the heaven, and for the beasts of the earth; and none shall fray them away. (Jeremiah 7:32–33; see Jeremiah 19:6; Isaiah.30:33)

Again, I am not saying hell does not exist. In fact, it very much does. It is a place where the sinner is waiting to be judged, a place of punishment which is brought on everyone who enters its doors.

What I am saying is that at the end of time (as we know it), death, hell, and those who are in them will be destroyed by the Lake of Fire. They will end and cease to be.

Until the Lake of Fire, those in hell will be tormented in ways beyond our comprehension. Their souls will be burning with a fire that cannot be quenched with any type of water we know of.

Another thing about hell: there is no kind of rest whatsoever. There will be no night and day. There will be no time (no seconds, minutes, hours, or days; no months, years, decades, or centuries). It will be constant. There will be no breaks of any kind. A person—or should I say your soul—will not be able to call for a time-out, to catch your breath (so to speak).

Their burning souls will never receive any kind of relief until they reach the Great White Throne Judgment.

I believe they will be tormented in such a harsh way, that when the end finally does come, they will willingly wish and want to be destroyed. They will be tormented in about the same way I was back in 1975.

Think about it.

Being in a place where you have all your senses but cannot use them. A place where nothing works except your mind (memory). A place where you know your destiny. A place without Jesus's love, grace, and mercy. A place of waiting. A place of loneliness. A place without peace of mind and soul.

You are all alone, in a place of loneliness, because this is personal.

And you are ashamed of yourself for being there.

You know, without any doubt whatsoever, that you are guilty and deserve punishment from God.

Not just a place of waiting for a few seconds, not just a few hours, like me, but a place of many days, months, and years.

A place of torment. What kind of torment? Of their own making.

Now, let me ask you this question.

Most of us can connect to this.

When you were a child, and you did something bad, and your mother caught you, instead of punishing you then, she looked at you and said, "Just wait until your dad gets home, and he will deal with you his way."

I do not know about you, but my dad knew how to use his belt quite well. It had a great stinging effect on the tail as well as on the mind. I dreaded his punishment, as well as waiting for it. I could not figure out which one was worse, the waiting or the punishment. What do you think?

Which would be worse for you, the waiting or the punishment? Most of us would say the waiting was worse. The waiting was a type of torment in our minds, wasn't it? A place for anticipating the upcoming punishment. A type of anxiety, in one way.

Now, keep this in mind. If you go to hell for rejecting Jesus, whose fault is it? It is not God's. It is not your family's or friends' fault. It is yours.

You will be tormenting yourself for being there.

You will be living and reliving your life over and over in your mind to see where you could have changed your circumstances and where your judgment could be changed for the better—knowing all along, there is no chance of that whatsoever. In hell, begging for forgiveness is useless. Forgiveness is not in hell. Forgiveness cannot be found in hell. Like it or not, forgiveness is for the living and not for the dead.

Those in hell know they are guilty, without any doubt, and are ashamed of it. To them knowing that the Lake of Fire lies ahead is a thought of relief, not a burden. Their burden will be meeting the Great Creator of the Universe without any excuses and knowing there is a price to be paid. With great shame, they will be anxiously waiting for the end of their existence. To them annihilation will be a merciful thought.

They will seek an end to stop their pain and torment. They will want it more than anything else. While in hell, sinners will reap what they sow during their lifetime on earth. In hell, the guilt of what they did in their lifetime will cause them to suffer tremendously. The greater their guilt, the greater their agony, and the more they will suffer. And the more they will wish for an end.

Psalm 9:17 says the wicked shall be turned into hell.

Let death seize upon them and let them go down quick [alive] into hell: for the wickedness is in their dwellings, and among them. (Psalm 55:15)

Proverbs 9:18 says that the foolish will go to hell. "**But he knoweth not that the dead are there and that her guests are in the depths of hell.**"

Now, who is the foolish? Those who reject God's gift to humanity. Proverbs 27:20 speaks about both hell and destruction. "**Hell** and destruction are never full, so the eyes of man are never satisfied." In other words, they are two separate ideas or places.

> And behold, one came and said unto him, Good Master, what good thing shall I do, that I may have eternal life? (Matthew 19:16)

> And these shall go away into everlasting punishment: but the righteous into life eternal. (Matthew 25:46)

> That whosoever believes in him should not perish but have eternal life. (John 3:16)

> And he that reap received wages and gather fruit unto life eternal. (John 4:36)

> Whoso eat my flesh, and drink my blood, hath eternal life. (John 6:54)

> Verily, verily, I say unto you, if a man keeps my saying, he shall never see death. (John 8:51)

> And I give unto them eternal life. (John 10:28)

> He that loves his life shall lose it, and he that hates his life in this world shall keep it unto life eternal. (John 12:25)

> As thou has given him power over the flesh, that he should give eternal life to as many as thou has given him. And this is life eternal, that they might know thee, the only true God. (John 17:2–3)

In other words, heaven is eternal and is full of life.
It never ends or has an ending of any kind.
It is not everlasting or forever, and that deals with time.
Eternal life goes beyond time.
Hell is a place of punishment and is everlasting, while heaven is eternal with abundance of life.

And being made perfect, he became the author of eternal salvation unto all them that obey him. (Hebrews 5:9)

In these verses, the Scripture states salvation is eternal. Not everlasting or forever; that deals with a limit or time.
Now, let us look at the definitions of hell.
There are four of them.

Gehenna, Geenna

Gehenna is the Latin word for the Hebrew term "Valley of Hinnom," which came to mean hell, along with *Topheth.*
It means "the place of punishment," as mentioned in Matthew 5:22, 29; 10:28; 18:9; 23:15, 33; Isaiah 33:14; 66:24; Mark 9:43; and Revelation 14:10; 20:10, 15; 21:8.

Tartarus

Next, *Tartarus* means the place of punishment, a place lower than *hades*, as mentioned in 2 Peter 2:4, the deepest abyss of hades.

Hades

Next, *hades* is the Greek word which means the place of the dead, as mentioned in Matthew 11:23; 16:18; Luke 16:23; Acts 2:27; and Revelation 1:18; 6:8; 20:13.

Sheol

Next, we have *Sheol*, which is the OT Hebrew word for *hades*, which also means the grave or unseen. It also means the realm of the dead. As mentioned in Deuteronomy 32:22; 2 Samuel 22:6; and Job 11:8; 26:6; Psalm 9:17; 16:10; 18:5; 55:15; 86:13; 116:3; 139:6; Proverbs 5:5; 7:27; 9:18; 15:11, 24; 23:14; 27:20; Isaiah 5:14; 14:9, 15; 28:15, 18; 57:9; Ezekiel 31:16; 32:21, 27; Amos 9:2; Jonah 2:2; and Habakkuk 2:5.

We also see the word *Pit* in the Scriptures. The Pit is usually referred to as *hades* or *Sheol*.

As I have already mentioned, there are thirteen different Hebrew words for the word *pit*.

There are other words for *pit* in the NT that refer to the *Abyss*.

Greek words for the pit are *phrear, abussos, bothynos,* and *borhtos*.

These words for *pit* were also used for certain demons that will be released during the tribulation period (Revelation 9:2, 11; 11:7; 17:8; 20:1)

There is another area called *under darkness* that is reserved for some other demons who left their first estate (Jude 6 and 2 Peter 2:4). It is also called *Tartarus*. This is the Old Testament word for the grave or the unseen and is seen in 1 Corinthians 55:55 as "O grave."

You also find "eternal fire," as mentioned in Matthew 3:12; 13:42; 18:8; 25:41; Mark 9:44; Luke 12:5; and James 3:6, which means burn up, furnace of fire, cut off, and everlasting punishment, as mentioned in Matthew 18:9; 25:41.

When we see damnation and perdition in the Scriptures, as we find in 2 Peter 2:4 and 3:7, they are referring to destruction, death, perish, and waste.

The word *hell* described in Revelation 20:13 means hades, which means place of the dead and the unseen, of departed souls, the grave.

Dead, in most areas of the Scriptures, means those who are torn away or separated from the living.

In other words, those who did not accept Jesus as their Savior will be completely separated from the living God because of their own sins.

> **Wherefore if thy hand or foot offend thee, cut them off, and cast them from thee. It is better for you to enter into life halted and maimed rather than having two hands or two feet to be cast into everlasting fire**. (Matthew 18:8)

"The fires of the soul are the unfulfilled desires and lusts, mental anguish, and burning memory of the foolish decision made in rejecting Almighty God." An anxiety type, multiplied many times.

Chapter 6

Hell Is Personal

Many believe that there will be crowds and great gatherings in the pits of hell. But that is as far from the truth as light is from darkness.

In my lifetime (which has been several years), I cannot count the times I heard someone say, "I will see you in hell." But that is not going to happen.

Even though hell had to enlarge its doors, there will be no crowds, gatherings, or meetings there.

> **Therefore, hell hath enlarged herself, and opened her mouth without measure; and their glory, and their multitude, and their pomp, and he that rejoiced, shall descend into it.**
>
> **And the mean man shall be brought down, and the mighty man shall be humbled, and the eyes of the lofty shall be humbled.** (Isaiah 5:14–15)

There will be no one to keep company with or to discuss any kind of matter. No friends or neighbors of any kind.

> **And there was certain rich man, which was clothed in purple and fine linen, and fared sumptuously every day.**

And there was a certain beggar named Lazarus, which was laid at his gate, full of sores,

And desiring to be fed with the crumbs which fell from the rich man's table; moreover, the dogs came and licked his sores.

And it came to pass that the beggar died and was carried by the angels into Abraham's bosom; the rich man also died and was buried.

And in hell, he lifted up his eyes, being in torment, and saw Abraham afar off, and Lazarus in his bosom.

And he cried and said, Father Abraham, have mercy on me, and send Lazarus, that he may dip the tip of his finger in water, and cool my tongue; for I am tormented in this flame.

But Abraham said, Son, remember that thou in thy lifetime receives thy good things; and likewise, Lazarus evil things; but now he is comforted and thou art tormented.

And beside all this, between you and us there is a great gulf fixed; so that they which would pass from hence to you cannot; neither can they pass to us, that would come from thence. (Luke 16:20–26)

In this passage of Scripture, there is no mention of others around the rich men. He is alone. He does not have any company. There is nobody or nothing to keep him company.

Why is it?

Why would God place him all alone? For one reason: hell is personal to each person who is in there. No one or anything else placed them there. The rich man chose to go there when he rejected God.

Everyone who ends up in hell has chosen to be placed there in one way or another. No one else can choose for you. It is your choice and yours only. Therefore, it is a very lonely place for reflection. A place of no encouragement. A place of no kind of support. A place of personal reflection, without any kind of interruption from anyone or anything else.

Also, in hell, the amount of torment is different from person to person. We find that mentioned in Luke concerning the rich man. The greater sins a person commits, the greater punishment or torments they will receive.

For it had been better for them not to have known the way of righteousness, than, after they have known it, to turn from the holy commandment delivered unto them. (2 Peter 2:21)

In other words, a harsher torment or punishment *awaits those* who commit greater sins. A different degree of torment.

Yes, even one sin will send a person to hell, but the more sins or greater sins a person commits, the greater the torment.

What will be the greater amount of punishment? You know, God is not subject to time. He created time. He can shorten time, lengthen time, extend time, or make time stand still. Who can say or cannot say, he will extend or shorten time in hell. To one, He may subject them to five hundred years in time, while others five thousand years; yet they both may take place at the same time. This is one way greater punishment can and may occur. This can be puzzling, I know. But our God can do anything.

However, no matter what degree of punishment and torment a person receives in hell, they will be alone and will suffer alone. They will have no one to keep them company or even try to ease their torment and torture.

Our sins are personal to God, just as our punishment for our sins will be personal to us in hell.

Regardless of what many claim and believe, there will also be nothing that will disturb and interrupt the pains and torments of hell. There will be no recess or breaks of any kind.

Remember, the rich man just wanted one drop of water to disturb his pain. But he did not get it. His pain and torment were constant and were connected to his life while living. His punishment was connected to what he did while living. He refused to give help to those in need, and he was refused help in hell. His remembrance of his life was a great part of his torments.

Therefore, his punishment in hell was personally connected to his sins while he was living.

After this earthly life, there will be no apologizing for sins committed or forgiveness of them. A person will see the sins they have committed and the reactions of their sins in their minds without any interruptions.

And they will know without any doubt that they are guilty and deserve death. Nobody will look at them and say something like, "Well, this other person did worse and look at him or her. They got off very lightly." No one will feel sorry for them and give them any kind of sympathy. A person in hell will know they deserve what they are getting and will receive later.

Again, hell is a place of loneliness. A type of torment and torture in itself. For most of us, being alone is unbearable and terrifying. We were made to have others around us. We may not think so, but we were and are.

If you do not believe this, just try to stay home for a week, without any kind of company. No visitors, no radios, no computers, no phones, and no television. You will find out very quickly, you were made to be around others. Without any kind of sensory feedback, most will become halfway loony. God made us not to be alone. This was just one reason He created Eve for Adam.

And the Lord God said, it is not good that the man should be alone; I will make him helps meet for him. (Genesis 2:18)

There is a reason we desire the input of others. Again, God made us that way. We were made for fellowship. We desire it and live for it.

One of the best descriptions of hell I heard from someone is described as: Being alone with nothing but your memories to keep you company is very, very frightening and moving.

Chapter 7

Misunderstandings

There are Scriptures that seem to show that hell may be eternal instead of everlasting.

Many believe that since several Scriptures say life is everlasting instead of eternal, hell must be eternal instead of everlasting.

As children of God, we need to always remember that life is not only everlasting, which is associated with time, as we know it, and has a limit, but eternity goes *beyond time*.

The souls of humans were not only meant to live in this world but were made to go beyond everlasting and enter into eternity. However, those who reject Christ as Lord will not see eternity. Christians will live beyond the time on this earth, but that is not so for the unsaved.

You find in the Bible, several Scriptures that seem to say hell is eternal, but let us look at them a little closer.

Here are some Scriptures which say we will receive everlasting life.

> **And everyone that hath forsaken houses, or brethren, or sisters, or father, or mother, or wife, or children, or lands, or lands, for my name's sake, shall receive a hundredfold and shall inherit *everlasting life*.** (Matthew 19:29)

Who shall not receive manifold more in this present time, and in the world to come *life everlasting.* (Luke 18:30)

For God so loved the world, that He gave His only begotten Son, that whosoever believes in Him, should not *perish*, but have *everlasting life.* (John 3:16)

He that believes on the Son hath *everlasting life*, but he that believe not the Son shall not see life, but the wrath of God abides on him. (John 3:36)

But whosoever drinks of the water that I shall give him shall never thirst, but the water that I shall give him shall be in him a well of water springing up into *everlasting life.* (John 4:14)

Verily, verily, I say unto you, he that hears my word and believes on Him that sent me, hath *everlasting life*, and shall not come into condemnation, but is passed from death unto life. (John 5:24)

Labor not for the meat which perishes, but for that meat which endures unto *everlasting life*, which the Son of man shall give unto you, for him hath God the Father sealed. (John 6:27)

And this is the will of Him that sent Me, that everyone who sees the Son and believes in Him, may have *everlasting life*, and I will raise him up at the last day. (John 6:40)

Verily, verily, I say unto you, he that believes in Me has *everlasting life.* (John 6:47)

And I know that his commandment is *life everlasting.* (John 12:50)

Then Paul and Barnabas waxed bold and said, it was necessary that the word of God should first have been spoken to you, but seeing ye put it from you, and judge yourselves unworthy of *everlasting life,* **we turn to the Gentiles.** (Acts 13:46)

But now being made free from sin, and you have your fruit unto holiness, and the end *everlasting life.* (Romans 6:22)

However, notice what it says in the next verse: "for the wages of sin is death, but the gift of God is *eternal life* through Jesus Christ our Lord."

Howbeit for this cause I obtained mercy, that in me first Jesus Christ might shew forth all longsuffering, for a pattern to them which should hereafter believe on Him to *life everlasting.* (1 Timothy 1:16)

The Greek word for "everlasting" at times will differ from what many believe.

The Greek word for "everlasting" is *aion* or *aionios,* which means a time period limited to age.

As I have already mentioned before, these words deal with time as we know it. As Christians, we should all know by now that we will receive not only everlasting life but eternal life as well.

However, the unforgiven sinner receives nothing of eternal means. They will receive no life whatsoever in hell, only misery and pain, and especially no eternal life.

No matter how many claim that hell is eternal and has no end, but that is not the case. Hell has an ending, as clearly stated in Revelation 20.

However, in many parts of the Scriptures, many believe that everlasting life and eternal life are the same, but look up their means.

Again, we need to understand that everlasting deals with a time period, has a limit, and does not go beyond that.

One reason many cannot get this right is that, as humans, we cannot really comprehend eternality, only time. We can, however, comprehend a little bit of everlasting because it deals with time as we know it.

We can deal with what we face daily, but to go beyond that, we are faced with things that are hard to comprehend and fathom. We can deal with time because we live and exist in time now. But to go beyond that is incomprehensible.

And like the old saying, that blows our minds.

Chapter 8

Hell Is Real

Hell is *real* and *not* some figment of somebody's imagination. It is as real as our everyday lives. It is more real than most of our experiences in life as we know it and must not be taken for granted.

Atheists do not believe in hell, because they do not believe in God. They tell themselves, if God does not exist, then hell does not exist. Therefore, why worry about something that doesn't exist? They believe in the concept of *"Do not worry about anything and live like you wish and desire."* Or at least until they are on their deathbed.

I am afraid this concept exists even inside a lot of our churches. Many inside our churches will claim that hell does not exist, and God's creation will be completely burned up in the Lake of Fire. But that is also not the case. They believe a righteous God like ours would not create anything as horrible as hell, to punish even the worst sinner. They cannot comprehend that God can do such a thing. They cannot comprehend the fact that our God can send or let anyone go to such a place. They claim eventually everyone will enter into the glory of heaven. Still others in our churches believe sinners will *not see* the pits of hell but cease to exist, after life in this world.

My friends, I am not saying or teaching that hell does not exist, but that it does have an ending. There are consequences for believing there is no such thing as hell.

Jesus spoke more about hell than almost any other type of subject, for a reason. One reason is that hell is full of pain and torment and deals with punishment of the soul. He warns many times, it is a place of suffering, a place of regrets. It is a place of sorrow, a place of waiting. Whether we like it or not, it is real and does exist, but praise God, one day it will be no more. One day, the last day, it will disappear into the "no-more." But for now, it is as real as life itself.

What happens in hell I have already explained to you in previous chapters. But I am here to explain to you that one day in the future, it will be annihilated, and everyone that is there now will be annihilated as well.

When is the end of hell? We will find that ending in Revelation 20:14–15, when we are told that "death and hell were cast into the lake of fire. This is the second death. And whosoever was not found written in the book of life was cast into the lake of fire."

Countless people over the centuries have asked, "What kind of fire exists in hell"? What will the sinners expect in hell? What kind of fire is the Lake of Fire? Is it the same kind of fire as in hell? Is there a difference? Like it or not, hell and the lake of fire are completely different from each other. One is the burning of the soul, while the other is an annihilation type.

But what exactly is the Lake of fire? As I have mentioned before, it is a consuming type of fire.

Psalms 55:23 says, "**But Thou of God shall bring them down into the pit of** *destruction*.**"**

It is a destructive type of fire. One that destroys, not prolongs.

Luke 3:17 states, "**Whose fan is in his hand, and he will thoroughly purge his floor, and will gather the wheat into his garner, but the chaff he will** *burn* **with fire unquenchable.**"

Who shall be punished with everlasting destruction from the presence of the Lord and from the glory of his power. (1 Thessalonians 1:9)

The Lord preserves all of them that love him, but all the wicked will he destroys. (Psalm 145:20)

Another explanation can be found in 2 Peter and in Jude7.

Even as Sodom and Gomorrah, and the cities about them in like manner, giving themselves over to fornication, are set forth for an *example*, suffering the vengeance of eternal fire. (Jude 7)

And turning the cities of Sodom and Gomorrah into ashes condemned them with an overthrow, making them an *ensample* unto those that after should live ungodly. (1 Peter 2:6)

Therefore, these verses show and tell us that the Lake of Fire is a destructive type of fire, not one that endures for eternity. It destroys, ends, and ceases to be.

Any unsaved person (sinner) who has not accepted Jesus as their Lord and Savior and dies today will enter the pits of hell very quickly.

Jesus spoke about hell many times, as I have mentioned in the other chapters:

- Matthew 5:22, 29–**30**; 7:13, 19; 8:12; 10:28; 11:23; 13:30, 40, 42, 49–50; 16:18; 18:8–9, 34; 22:13; 23:14–15, **33**; 24:51; 25:30, 41, 46;
- Mark 3:29; 9:43–48; 12:40;
- Luke 3:17; 10:15; 12:5, 46–48; 16:23–26; 20:47;
- John 5:29; 15:6.

Today, as in the past, there are many groups which claim hell is a figment of someone's imagination.

Many have claimed that hell is an idea made up by certain people, to scare individuals into doing their bidding. And we do not need to pay any attention to those who say that the Bible is a book created by man to force humankind to do their bidding, and God had no part in it. These are those who never open the Bible and are easily persuaded. They desire to do their own bidding, without accepting any consequences of their own. They want all that life can give and are not willing to give anything in return. They believe they can do what they desire and live the way of the world, overlooking what really lies ahead of them. They can be found in every community, every town, every city, and every country. They are everywhere. And it will be those who will probably be the first ones to enter the doors of hell. They will never give reverence to God and His people and never believe they will.

But God's Word contradicts that, as mentioned in Romans 14:11: **"For it is written, As I live, saith the LORD, every knee shall bow to me, and every tongue shall confess to God."**

One day, everyone will believe in God, and one day, all who fail to accept Jesus as their Lord will enter the doors of hell to pay for their disbelief and atone for their sins.

I would like to ask this: "How many in our world today have not heard of our God and Jesus Christ in one way or another?" They may not have accepted Him as their Lord and Savior, but almost everyone has heard of Him.

Many claim God as their Almighty Creator, but nothing else. They believe that He offers no existence after death. But why does He give us His Word that is different and full of love and mercy and warnings for rejecting it? Why does He even care if we love Him or not?

Many feel that there is no life after death, one way or another. I do not know about you, but it would scare the living daylights out of me if I believed that.

If I believed that, when a person dies, they return to dust, and their existence disappears into the wind, that would in a way scare me. That's a hard idea to fathom. Again, what would scare a person more, the thought of going to hell or being erased from existence altogether? Especially if they may be an atheist.

Regardless of whether we believe it or not, God has placed inside each of us a light and a knowledge that tells us that there is a great, loving God who offers life after death. He cares and loves humanity, more than anyone can comprehend. And He has given us His Word to back that up, as well as for the punishment of unbelievers. Otherwise, what would be the use of living if this is all there is?

Regardless of what many believe and claim, everyone knows there is something else after death. Life or hell. Life does not end in death and the grave. However, it does for the sinner, at the Great White Throne.

Many believe in reincarnation—that a soul lives on and on throughout many lifetimes, and that it just spontaneously lives on. And that God has no dealing in human life whatsoever. This is almost as bad as those who do not believe in God and believe there no such thing as hell.

Many beliefs of this world deny the existence of God and Jesus Christ, and life after death. Many claim that hell is a way to keep people under submission and to scare them in one way or another. They claim that it is a figment of someone's imagination.

Satan would have us to believe these kinds of things. He knows that by keeping people from the knowledge of God' s future for mankind, he may influence many to join him in hell and the lake of fire.

He knows that by influencing humanity to overlook God's love for them and the existence of hell, he would undoubtedly send them to hell, to hurt God's feelings. He does not care about except doing harm to our God. He knows he is doomed, and he wants to take as many as he can to hell right along with him.

I cannot comprehend the idea of *no hell*, any more than denying the existence of God. God tells us and warns us about hell and its existence throughout His holy Word. Hell exists and is very much real. This is why He warns us of its punishments that await each person who rejects His love and sacrifice.

He speaks quite often in the Scriptures of atonement and punishment for a reason. Atonement and punishment exist in the pits of hell, not in someone's imagination, as many have claimed and continue to claim.

When time ends, at the Great White Throne Judgment and on the last day of time, all unforgiven sinners will be annihilated, destroyed, and cease to be. As stated in Revelation, all those in hell will be cast into the Lake of Fire, an eternal fire that consumes and demolishes.

The question is, where will you be that day?

Chapter 9

Is God in Hell?

Now, another good question many have asked: "Is God in hell today?"

Does God have to be in hell for hell to exist? We all have heard God is everywhere, right? The Scriptures describe Him *as Omnipresent*. He is everywhere, at any moment. He is in the past, He is in the now, and He is in the future. He is in the earth, He is in the sky, He is in the stars, He is in the land, He is in the oceans, He is in all the planets, He is in the moon—and yes, He is in hell.

There is no place where He is not. His Word tells us that He is everywhere. There is no place that exists where He is not there.

To say anything different is to call God a liar. And we know He is not. He must be and must be everywhere, or those places will cease to be.

Again, with this in mind, is God in hell right now? What do you think?

What does Psalm 139:7–8 say? "**Whither shall I go from thy spirit? Or whither shall I flee from thy presence? If I ascend up into heaven, thou are there; if I make my bed in hell (*Sheol*), thou are there.**"

Are the Scriptures wrong?

I have heard it said that He cannot be in hell, and God is not in hell. However, He must be in hell if hell exists.

Regardless, if we believe it or not, nothing can exist without

God. Take God out of anything, and it ends immediately. Where He is, life exists, or should I say, there is existence. There can be nothing, if God is not there. He is life, and life exists in Him. He is not the God of nothingness.

Again, I have heard many say that only God's essence is there, for the existence of hell, but not Him personally. But the question is, "If His essence is there, isn't He there?"

Whether we like it or not, take God out of hell, and hell would cease to be. No two ways about it. He created hell for Satan and his followers. But humankind seems to enjoy following their leader (Satan) himself, as far as even the pits of hell.

Our God knows those in hell and what they are doing. He knows their torment and pain. However, He does not take pleasure for those in that place. Even though humanity *was not destined* to walk through the doors of hell, they will end up there for rejecting the greatest Savior of humankind (Jesus Christ). But have no doubt about it, God is in hell, right now, and must be, if it is to endure and exist.

Again, like it or not, He must be there. Without God, hell would cease to be. No two ways about it.

Again, what would happen if God were taken out of some place? It ceases to be.

The eyes of the LORD are in every place, beholding the evil and the good. (Proverbs 15:3)

Can any hide himself in secret places that I shall not see him? Said the LORD. Do not I fill heaven and earth? Said the LORD. (Jeremiah 23:24)

That they should seek the Lord if happily they might feel after Him, and find Him, though He is not far from every one of us. (Acts 17:27)

Again, I cannot count the times I have heard people and even many Christians claim, "God is not in hell." I have heard even preachers tell me that. They cannot understand that He must be. Take God out of any place, and that place would simply cease to be.

You may say and think God cannot be in hell, because He is a God of love and righteousness, and there is none of that in hell. Yes, that is right. I know it is hard to understand and comprehend that right now. But He must be there for hell to exist. I don't understand it, but maybe one day I will, if He desires it.

Now, I am not saying his righteousness is in hell. I don't know, but He must have some kind of essence there for it to even exist and endure.

God is everywhere. He is *omnipresent*. Nothing and no one else is. But He is. Take God out of anything and anywhere, and it will simply cease to be.

Now, another question one may ask is "Will God spend eternity in hell for that place to exist?"

Again, remember, take God out of anywhere, and it will cease to be. Nothing can exist without Him.

This is why God says, in Revelation, "*Death and hell* will be *cast into* the lake of fire." Not into another hell or continuing hell, or another place of torture and torment, but the Lake of Fire.

Because the Lake of Fire is a place of consumption and destruction. A place of annihilation and ending. In other words, it is a place of destruction, as most of us may understand. As I have already mentioned many times before.

As I mentioned before in this book, the second death is the *destruction of the souls* of the sinners. Not a continuation of punishment. It is an ending. It is their end.

It is not hell (*Sheol*, the realm of the dead) or (*hades*, which is the same place. It is not a waiting area of punishment and suffering.

The Lake of Fire is not another type of hell. It is a place of complete and final destruction. An ending. An annihilation.

By this, we see and find, that our God will not watch the continued punishment of all sinners. He watches them as they spend time in hell, but when time ends, even though sinful people chose to go into hell in the first place, there existence will end.

We know that to be true, because of the parable of Lazarus and the rich man.

But to watch their suffering throughout eternity—what would be the purpose of it? He does not take any kind of delight in watching sinners suffer. He never did and never will.

This is why He offered salvation through His Son, Jesus Christ. Over and over again, God warns humanity of the consequences of sin, with His Word and Scriptures. Still, many have and will still overlook His Word and choose their own way, or should I say, Satan's way.

Chapter 10

The Lake of Fire, the End of All Things

What exactly is the Lake of Fire? Is it a continuation of hell? Is it another word for hell? No!

It is a destructive type of fire, an annihilation type, and an ending type. One that ends all things. It is like a piece of paper being held over a lit match. It consumes and destroys.

This is why the Lake of Fire is at the end of life in this world. To end all suffering, eternally, once and for all. Even for those who deserve it and choose it

An end to all punishment, pain, sorrows, and torment. Even for those who deserve it. Even for those who choose it.

Now, what happens *after* the end?

Read what Revelation 21:5 says: "And God shall wipe away all tears from their eyes; and there shall be no more death, neither sorrow, nor crying, neither shall there be any more pain; for the former things are *passed away*."

And He said this *after* the evil was cast into the Lake of Fire, not before.

Not only does our Creator provide everyone with salvation and escape from any kind of torment; *He ends all punishment* once and for all. That alone should enlighten our souls as children of Almighty God. All those we love now, as in the past, who rejected Christ as Lord and King, will one day have an end to their suffering. We all have had somebody we loved in our past who didn't claim Jesus as their Lord, and died without Him. Most of us today have friends and loved ones, who still have not accepted Him. Do we wish to see them suffer eternally? No. The same can be said about God. He does not desire to see anyone suffer.

God has never taken delight in suffering, especially that of humankind.

And He bestowed that compassion and emotion upon all humankind as well. For the most part, we avoid suffering, not only for ourselves but for others and other living things as well.

Let me ask you this. What do you do when you see some animal suffering? You want to relieve its suffering, don't you? What do you do if you see a dog or cat get run over, especially your own pet? You try to help it or take it to someone to receive help.

But what if it is beyond help? Do you watch it suffer until it dies? Or would you try to put it out of its misery? Why do we care if something is suffering? Did we learn that someplace in life?

Were we born with compassion? I believe so.

I know, many never seem to have any form of compassion, but for the most part, we all have some kind of compassion and emotions when it comes to suffering.

I have seen several friends in my lifetime who had some kind of illness, which caused a great deal of suffering. When this happens to someone I know or love, I would do almost anything to see them receive relief—sometimes to the point of hoping they would go ahead and pass away and end their pain.

Is this something we should be worried about? No!

Are we wrong in thinking and wanting that, when there is nothing else we can do? No. If so, where do our compassion and emotions come from? From God.

Just like the desire to seek God and His love was placed in us when He created us, so were our compassion and emotions, or should I say His.

With this in mind, do you think and feel God would watch the sufferings of fallen humankind for eternity? I believe not, but what do you believe? What do you think?

This is why we read in Revelation 21:4 that "**God shall wipe away all tears from their eyes; and there shall be no more death, neither sorrow, nor crying, neither shall there be any more pain: for the former things are** *passed away.*"

In other words, *no more suffering* of any kind. All sufferings end at the Great White Throne. No more pains of any kind. No more regrets whatsoever. No more remembering past losses, because all unforgiven sinners are no more (regardless of whether they may be your brothers, sisters, fathers, mothers, cousins, grandparents, friends, or any other relation). Their existence has ceased to be. Their suffering has ended. They are no longer in pain and misery.

Therefore, what would be the purpose of remembering and mourning for them? They will become memories for you to use later. All their experiences and your memories of them (both good and bad) can be drawn upon and used later on, not forgotten.

Many believe God will wipe away our memories when we leave this world. Because they believe and feel that if they knew someone who descended into hell, they would not be happy at all.

I like to ask this question: "Why would God wipe our memories and start us on a clean slate?" Why would He erase from our brains all the memories of past victories, heartaches, pains, and the suffering we had and start us on a new road or path of life? Why would He take those memories away?

If He wiped our memories clean, we would have no idea how or why we are in heaven. My friends, He will never take away our memories of accepting Jesus as Lord and King. He wants us to know why we are there. He wants us to know why He allowed us in heaven. If He took those memories away, could we love Him as much as we could? Could we love Him if we don't know why we should?

He could have made us like robots to start with, to do His bidding, but He did not. He gave us free will and wants us to know that we also choose Him through His Son, Jesus. Besides that, what would be the purpose of taking our memories of our lives and experiences and casting them to the side? Do we not learn from our mistakes? For the most part, we learn the most from our past mistakes, pains, and sufferings. They make us who we are. They form our general opinions in life. They form our reason to live, our way of living and thinking, and our ability to associate with others and especially God.

Did He not say in the Scriptures that we shall judge the worldly matters? **"Do you not know that the saints shall judge the world? And the world shall be judged by you, are ye unworthy to judge the smallest matters?"** (1 Corinthians 6:2).

Where will we receive that knowledge to do so? From our experiences in our lifetimes. From our past history, both bad and good. Without our memories of our past experiences, sufferings, victories, pains, and troubles, we will not qualify to be any kind of judges. Therefore, our memories are and will be important to our God.

Therefore, we need to keep in mind that out God is not only going to let us keep our memories but provides us a way to let the memories of our lost one not affect us by ending the existence of those who refuse God's salvation, right along with their suffering and pains, once and for all.

God Himself is not going to deal with and watch suffering through eternity. So ending the existence of those who rejected His salvation also provides a way for His saints to do the same—even though they may know some who went to hell and were destroyed.

Manu claims that heaven could not be heaven if its residents knew some of their loved ones were tormented in the pits of hell. The Lake of Fire will end of sufferings, pains, and torment from all existences whatsoever.

He is a God of love. He is a God of compassion.

He is a God of forgiveness.

He is a God who loves and cares for His creation. Not one who enjoys watching His creation suffer.

Conclusion

Today, we see and find many beliefs on what happens after death. Almost everyone wonders what happens after death. There are many thoughts of what kind of life one may find in heaven and what one may expect in hell.

Almost everyone wonders exactly what takes place in hell.

In Luke we find Jesus speaking about Lazarus and the rich man in hell. What was the rich man doing in hell? He was not just visiting with his family and friends. In fact, he was completely alone.

But what was he doing, besides crying out to God.

Almost everyone has heard that old saying, "I'll see you in hell," but the question is, will we? What kind of life or existence is there in hell? What lies beyond hell? Is hell eternal, without any kind of end, and if it has an ending, when does it occur?

What does God's holy Word say about it? What will the atheist and sinner have to look forward to? What will those denominations or cults who have rejected Jesus as their Savior have to look forward to?

Does life or existence exist beyond death and the grave for everyone?

After the Great White Throne Judgment and immediately upon sentencing, Satan, his angels, and his human followers receive their punishment.

They are to die an eternal death. They are cast into the Lake of Fire. Eternal annihilation. Eternal destruction.

As well as Satan and his followers, the Lake of Fire will devour and destroy all the unsaved.

Revelation tells us, if a person's name is not found in the Book of Life, they will be cast into the Lake of Fire.

Like Satan and his followers, every sinner will be annihilated and destroyed. The devil and his associates, and all sinners will also suffer this fate.

The context of the entire Bible makes clear that the second death mentioned in Revelation 21:8 means the wicked will suffer their annihilation, their total destruction.

But the fearful, and unbelieving, and the abominable, and murderers, and whoremongers, and sorcerers, and idolaters, and all liars, shall have their part in the lake which *burneth* with fire and brimstone, which is the second death. (Revelation 21:8)

What, then, is the concept of eternally burning hell?

As we see in this book and other studies, Scripture teaches no such place.

Biblically, hell is the place and state of punishment in time, as we know it.

Most Bibles use the word "hell" to translate the Hebrew word *Sheol* and the Greek *hades*. These terms generally refer to the grave where the dead (both righteous and wicked) await in a state of unconsciousness until the resurrection or Judgment.

In contrast, the Greek word *Geenna* or *Gehenna* denotes a *waiting place* for fiery punishment.

Geenna is derived from the Hebrew Ge Hinnom, valley of Hinnom, a gorge on the south side of Jerusalem.

Here, Israel had conducted the heathen rite of burning children to Molech, as stated in 2 Chronicles 28:3.

Jeremiah predicted that because of this sin, the LORD would make the valley a "Valley of Slaughter," where the corpses of the Israelites would be buried till there was no more place for them. The remaining bodies were to be food for the birds (Jeremiah. 7:32–33).

Jeremiah's prophecy undoubtedly led Israel to view Ge Hinnom as a place of judgment of the wicked, a place of abhorrence, punishment, and shame.

Later, rabbinical tradition considered it a place for burning carcasses and rubbish.

> Ahaz was twenty years old when he began to reign sixteen years in Jerusalem; but he did not that which was right in the sight of the LORD, like David, his father.
>
> For he walked in the ways of the kings of Israel and also made molten images for Baalim.
>
> Moreover, he burnt incense in the valley of the son of Hinnom and burnt his children in the fire after the abominations of the heathen whom the LORD had cast out before the children of Israel. (2 Chronicles 28:1–3)
>
> Manasseh was twelve years old when he began to reign and reigned fifty-and-five years in Jerusalem.
>
> But did that which was evil in the sight of the LORD, like unto the abominations of the heathen, whom the LORD had cast out before the children of Israel.
>
> For he built again the high places which Hezekiah his father had broken down, reared up altars for Balaam, made groves, worshipped all the host of heavens, and served them.
>
> Also, he built altars in the house of the LORD, whereof the LORD had said, In Jerusalem shall my name be forever."
>
> And he built altars for all the host of heaven in the two courts of the house of the LORD.
>
> And he caused his children to pass through the fire in the valley of the son of Hinnom;

also, he observed times, used enchantments, and dealt with a familiar spirit and wizards; he wrought much evil in the sight of the LORD, to provoke him to anger. (2 Chronicles 33:1–6)

Therefore, behold, the days come, saith the LORD, that it shall no more be called Tophet, nor the valley of the son of Hinnom, but the valley slaughter; for they shall bury in Tophet, till there be no place.

And the carcasses of this people shall be meat for the fowls of the heaven, and for the beasts of the earth; and none shall fray them away. (Jeremiah 7:32–33; see Jeremiah 19:6; Isaiah 30:33)

Jesus used the fires of Hinnom as a representation of hellfire (Matthew 5:22). Therefore, the fires of Hinnom symbolized the consuming fire of the last judgment. He stated that it was an experience beyond death (Luke 12:5) and that hell would destroy both body and soul, as stated in Matthew 10:28.

But I say unto you, that whosoever is angry with his brother without a cause shall be in danger of the judgment; and whosoever shall say to his brother, Raca, shall be in danger of the council; but whosoever shall, thou fool, shall be in danger of hell fire. (Matthew 5:22)

And if thine eye offends thee, pluck it out, and cast it from thee; it is better for thee to enter into life with one eye, rather than having two eyes to be cast into hell fire. (Matthew 18:9)

But I will forewarn you whom ye shall fear; Fear him, which after he hath killed hath power

**to cast into hell; yea, I say unto you, fear him.
(Luke 12:5)**

**And fear not them which kill the body but are
not able to kill the soul; but rather fear him
which is able to *destroy both* body and soul in
hell.** (Matthew 10:28)

Therefore, what is the nature of hellfire?

Do unsaved sinners exist in hell burn eternally? No!

According to the Scriptures, God promises eternal life and existence only to the righteous.

The wages of sin is death, not eternal life and existence in hell.

The Scriptures teach that the wicked will be cut off (Psalm 37:20) and that they will perish (Psalm 37:20; 68:2).

And they will not live eternally in a state of consciousness but will be burned up, consumed, destroyed, annihilated (Malachi 4:1; Matthew 13:30, 40; 2 Peter 3:10).

They will be destroyed (Psalm 145:20; 2 Thessalonians 1:9) and consumed (Psalm 104:35).

**But the wicked *shall perish*, and the enemies of
the LORD shall be as the fat of lambs; they shall
consume; into smoke shall they *consume away*.**
(Psalm 37:20)

**As smoke is driven away, so drive them away;
as wax melt before the fire, so let the wicked
perish in the presence of God.** (Psalm 68:2)

**For, behold, the day cometh, that shall burn
as an oven; and all the proud, yea, and all that
do wickedly, shall be stubble; and the day that
cometh shall *burn* them up, saith the LORD of**

hosts, that it shall leave them neither root nor branch. (Malachi 4:1)

Let them grow together until the harvest, and in the time of harvest I will say to the reapers, gather ye together first the tares, and bind them in bundles to *burn* them, but gather the wheat into my barn. (Matthew 13:30)

As therefore the tares are gathered and *burned* in the fire, so shall it be at the end of this world. (Matthew 13:40)

But the day of the Lord will come as a thief in the night, in the which the heaven shall pass away with a great noise, and the elements shall melt with fervent heat, the earth also and the works that are therein shall be *burned up*. (2 Peter 3:10)

The LORD preserves all of them that love him, but all the wicked will he *destroy*. (Psalm 145:20)

Who shall be punished with everlasting *destruction* from the presence of the Lord and from the glory of his power. (2 Thessalonians 1:9)

Forasmuch then as the children are partakers of flesh and blood, he also himself likewise took part of the same; that through death he might *destroy* him that had the power of death, that is, the devil. (Hebrews 2:14)

Hell deals with the existence of time.

Take, for example, Jude 7, which tells of the fate of Sodom and Gomorrah. They suffered the vengeance of eternal fire. Yet those cities are not burning today. They were completely annihilated.

Peter said that that fire turned those cities into ashes, condemning them to destruction (2 Peter 2:6). Eternal fire (Lake of Fire) burns *until* there is nothing left to burn, and then it goes out.

As with any type of fire we know today, it destroys and turns substance into nothing but ashes to blow away with the wind. But the fires of hell are different from anything we know.

The fire in hell is different than the type of fire of the Lake of Fire. It is the fire of the soul, an anxiety type of fire, which is much worse than anything we can imagine. It sets the soul and mind with a type of fire that is unbearable.

As I mentioned before, the Webster dictionary describes anxiety as "a painful or apprehensive of mind, an impending or anticipated ill. Fearful concern or interest. An abnormal and overwhelming sense of apprehension and fear often marked by physiological signs (as sweeting, tensions, and increased pulse) of doubt concerning the reality and nature of the threat and by self-doubt about one's capacity to cope."

Again, remember, the fires of the soul are the unfulfilled desires and lusts, mental anguish, and burning memory of the foolish decisions made in rejecting Almighty God.

Hellfire is the *burning of the souls* and not physical bodies. It is *completely different* from any kind of pain our physical bodies can endure, and it exists in time.

But the type of fire at the end (the Lake of Fire) is a consuming, destructive one that annihilates, that ends everything. It ends the existence of all sinful life, even time itself.

Before I end this book, I would like to look into the Scriptures of Ezekiel again and see what God will do to Satan in Ezekiel 28:14–19:

Thou art the anointed cherub that covereth; and I have set thee; thou wast upon the holy

85

mountain of God; thou hast walked up and down in the midst of the stones of fire.

Thou wast perfect in thy ways from the day that thou wast created, till iniquity was found in thee.

By the multitude of thy merchandise they have filled the midst of thee with violence, and thou hast sinned: therefore, I will cast thee as profane out of the mountain of God; I will *destroy thee*, O covering cherub, from the midst of the stones of fire.

Thine heart was lifted up because of thy beauty, thou hast corrupted thy wisdom by reason of thy brightness; I will cast thee to the ground, I will lay thee before kings, that they may behold thee.

Thou hast defiled thy sanctuaries by the multitude of thine iniquities, by the iniquity of thy traffick; therefore, will I bring forth a fire from the midst of thee, it shall *devour thee*, and I will *bring thee to ashes* upon the earth in the sight of all them that behold thee.

All they that know thee among the people shall be astonished at thee; thou shalt be a terror, and *never shalt thou be anymore.*

By this Scripture in Ezekiel, we see that at the very end, Satan will be completely annihilated, consumed, destroyed, and turned to ashes. He is not destined to spend eternity in hell but will be destroyed. His existence will end. He will cease to be.

In Revelation, we see him cast into the Lake of Fire, to be destroyed as mentioned in Ezekiel, and after that the rest of fallen humanity to join him. They will be no more. Nada, nothing. They will be annihilated, consumed, and destroyed, once and for all, throughout all eternity. Never to exist ever again in any kind of way.

But still, I question those who believe hell is eternal. Why do they hold on to that idea, while the Scriptures tell and explain something different? Why are certain words and Scriptures overlooked? I tend to look at it this way: like many I have known in the past, who believe that if King James English was good enough for Peter and Paul, it must and should be good enough for me. In other words, they go along with the status quo. It was taught to them that way, and it must be right. If Brother so-and-so or Sister so-and-so said it, it must be true. They never question what has been taught and told to them in the past. This is why we, as children of God, need to study God's words for ourselves and question their meanings.

Therefore, I challenge everyone who reads this book to personally research God's holy words. Do not take my word to be true, or anyone else's. Study for yourselves, search the Scriptures, and pray for discernment and understanding.

Remember, every one of us is a *human being.* We all make mistakes, and we all are sinners. Even though we may be saved by the grace of God, we still fall short in our daily lives. However, God's Word never fails. It never disappoints. His words will live on throughout eternity, while ours will not. God is the source of all knowledge and power, which will never, never end. He is the omnipotent, omnipresent, and omniscient God. He is the all-powerful, all-present, and all-knowing, God. Everything comes from Him. Everything exists because of Him. He is the nourisher and sustainer of all life. Without Him, nothing can exist.

Printed in the United States
by Baker & Taylor Publisher Services